CREATING YOUR CAREER

PRACTICAL ADVICE FOR GRADUATES IN A CHANGING WORLD

SIMON KENT

**KOGAN
PAGE**

First published in 1997

Kogan Page Limited
120 Pentonville Road
London N1 9JN

British Library Cataloguing in Publication Data

A CIP record for this book is available from the British Library.

ISBN 0 7494 2040 5

Designed and typeset by Kate Williams
Printed and bound in Great Britain by Clays Ltd, St Ives plc

CONTENTS

PART THREE

CASE STUDIES

PREFACE

In the past few years I have met hundreds of people in diverse work situations and asked them what they do, why they do it, how they got to do it in the first place and what they want to do next.

The answer to the first question is usually self-evident. The second question is less easy, but in general happily employed people – from retail managers, to North Sea oil workers, to mortuary technicians – find that work is a part of their lives rather than apart from their lives. What they do genuinely interests them, provides a wide variety of stimuli and is not simply a support mechanism.

The final two questions produce increasingly weird and wonderful responses. Employment in all sectors is unpredictable and professional workers often find themselves at the mercy of a volatile economy and fashionable management techniques. On one occasion I met a chiropodist who, prior to redundancy, worked for many years as an aircraft engineer. Despite this immense change, he found his new occupation provided a good standard of living – not purely through financial reward – but because he could now work the hours he wanted in his local area.

You have a choice. Accept that the career is dead or create your own. Take whatever work comes your way in the hope that it will satisfy you over some period of time, or identify what you want out of the workplace and find a way to fulfil those requirements. You will not find the right work by ticking job checklists or answering personality questionnaires. You must take the initiative: identify what you want, exploit the opportunities you have and create your career the way you want it to be.

INTRODUCTION

Considering your future is never an easy or comfortable task, but in today's job market it is imperative that every worker, in or out of employment, maintains a clear focus on what they want to do for a living. Financial demands for immediate survival needs can force bad career decisions. College life tends to be learning- rather than career-oriented and the approach of finals can be all consuming. Many students experience problems as they do not consider their first career move until after graduation. Indeed, some graduates and professionals find themselves drifting into their first job, or between jobs, without any coherent structure.

For those in professional work, job dissatisfaction or threats of redundancy can make working life miserable. Without a definitive Plan A (let alone an acceptable Plan B), alternative arrangements are impossible to consider. What you do for a living dictates many other aspects of your life – financial remuneration, free time and future prospects. It is therefore imperative that you create a career for yourself, as dissatisfaction here will affect the rest of your life.

Pursuing a chosen line of work presents particular problems today. The pathway to full-time professional employment is no longer clearly defined. To begin with, areas of work have altered. The UK's manufacturing base has been decimated with many traditional industries disappearing, swamped by foreign competitors, or radically restructured through privatisation or the influence of the stock-market. The demise of large industries has had a knock-on effect throughout the economy, putting some companies out of business, signalling restructure in others and promoting uncertainty all round.

The type of work people do has changed and continues to do so at an increasing speed. Information technology is the latest element in the ongoing process of evolving and improving work practices. Technology has revolutionised the workplace from the production line to the banks. Modern offices have scant need for secretarial staff since management can wordprocess their own material in the same amount of time. Secretarial positions have metamorphosed into Personal Assistant roles, taking on more administrative duties and responsibilities, which frequently require a graduate education.

The recession led organisations to exploit any opportunity to get more work done with fewer resources. Private companies and public institutions have all cut back expenditure and since the highest cost to a business is payroll, 'down-sizing' or, more acceptably, 'right-sizing' the workforce has become very popular. Entire levels of middle management have been stripped out and the staff who remain have found their responsibilities expanding to take up the slack. The old hierarchical structures have been flattened to produce faster communications and more flexibility within businesses. Flexibility has also led to short-term and project-based contracts enabling organisations to take on and drop workers as and when required.

Graduates and job-seeking professionals will need to understand these new working structures in order to find ways into satisfying occupations. If you are able to negotiate and utilise these new structures you will be able to work in any area of employment.

Companies need young, highly skilled people to operate in and influence the commercial world. Indeed, some competition is beginning to emerge between companies to attract the best candidates. Skill shortages are emerging in the workforce, particularly in engineering and science, but on the whole the job market remains a buyer's market where employers call the shots and stipulate precise recruitment requirements.

There are many myths surrounding the recruiting processes of some employers. With a large response to every advertisement, primary selection can be based on grounds unrelated to the position advertised. Applications arriving by second class post may be excluded. Selection can occur on the basis of GCSE results. Other companies use computer technology to scan and select CVs on the basis of key words or phrases. This is something to bear in mind when preparing your own.

Job-hunting includes as much luck as skill. This book details only some of the ways in which companies recruit and ways in which you can find the position that suits you. The often quoted cliché, 'It's not what you know, it's who you know', is particularly true today, where being in the right place at the right time and knowing the right person is likely to get you more work than sending off hundreds of copies of your CV, hoping one will land on the right desk. But this is not to say that sending off your CV speculatively will not secure your perfect job.

Once you have secured employment you cannot expect your employer to look after you for the rest of your working life. There are very few complete career paths in existence and most employers cannot develop, train or promote their employees. Many will be unable to specify or guarantee the length of your employment. It is up to you to create your own long-term career plan. This entails deciding what to do for a living, where to do it and what the rewards will be.

Managing your own career requires certain skills, which the Association of Graduate Recruiters has described as 'self-reliance skills'. In effect, the individual provides the support structures that were previously provided by employers in the traditional career structure. While these are relatively new responsibilities for professional workers, many graduates have used similar skills at college. Increased class sizes mean students have had to organise their own study and achieve self-set targets within time restrictions with little tutorial support, be it a dissertation, an essay or presentation. The ability to arrange your work and social life, motivate yourself and complete projects is just as important in the workplace.

Your career will be as individual and unique as you are. There are no set routes, so in order to make the most of the new work structures it is important to recognise your skills and strengths, and to know the way you want to work and the area in which you want to operate. It is these factors, rather than an employer's expectations or company structure, that will guide you from one activity to the next.

This book is not a prescriptive 'look it up' reference book. It is a sort of map detailing the world of work and suggesting how to find your way around it. Part One describes the current patterns of working life. In Part Two there are overviews of selected areas of employment. Part Three encourages you to assess your own skills, identify your aims and unite the two in order to create your career.

It is worth remembering that decisions you take now will not dictate what you do for the rest of your life. Many graduates change jobs after the first two years having gained a clearer idea of what they want to do and what is available. You may find your dream job is not as good as you first thought or that new technology completely changes your task. Today's professional worker should expect to work for many employers throughout their career in a wide variety of situations. This arrangement can offer more satisfying work than the traditional career structure of the single employer. If you have the skills employers need and the determination to succeed you will create a career that always provides great satisfaction, working in many different places and situations in a rewarding way.

PART ONE

HOW TO WORK

The area in which you work is entirely your own choice but you have less control over how that work is arranged. Working hours and other employment conditions are all your employers' prerogative, although you or a representative body, such as a union or association, may be able to influence the contract. However, there are some changes in career patterns and the relationship between employer and employee that are out of everyone's control.

Employing graduates and professionals used to be a straightforward process. Employers would meet graduates towards the end of their student life, perhaps at a careers fair, presentation or during the Milk Round. The graduate would apply, be interviewed and, if suitable, recruited onto a graduate trainee course. Employment meant working for one organisation for a number of years, and rising through the ranks gaining promotion with increased responsibility and remuneration. Once employed, few graduates found themselves unemployed and so effectively had the security of a job for life. Low job satisfaction, low remuneration or offers of better employment were the only reasons a professional might change jobs.

It is still possible to follow this employment model. Individual employers in some areas of employment are able to offer satisfying work and a structured career ladder. More commonly, however, organisations cannot offer continual development for their employees. While harsh economic conditions have contributed to these changes, the way work is done has evolved from being role based to project led. Instead of employing someone indefinitely to carry out a general task on a day-to-day basis, staff are employed to work towards a specific short-term goal.

The trend suggests workers in the future will be employed in a wide range of scenarios by a number of employers. They may switch between a number of regular employers throughout the year, or work for more than one employer at any one time. Work may last months or weeks but eventually the employee will have to find a new job. This does not mean that the workforce of the future will be entirely made up of freelance self-employed workers but there are many elements of this style of working that will prove useful to negotiating the job market of the future.

Some practitioners describe the new model as the 'portfolio career'. As the name implies, a career such as this contains many different tasks and working skills. The strength of the portfolio career lies in its diversity. A wide range of skills increases the number of jobs you can apply for and your attractiveness for an employer.

Your own career will probably be somewhere between the traditional and portfolio models. To some extent, how you work will depend on the industry and company you enter. As time goes by it is more likely you will need the career management skills of the portfolio career rather than the disciplines of the traditional career.

From job for life to portfolio career

Dawn Johnson had worked in a national government office for 18 years when she was made redundant as part of its restructuring programme. She had risen to the position of head of marketing and publicity and become, she says, 'part of the furniture'. As part of her redundancy package she was given careers advice from a firm of professional careers consultants. Prior to her sessions with the consultants she believed she would find it difficult to find work in another company because her experience, although extensive, was narrow in focus. The careers consultants helped her to clarify how she could work in today's market. They identified the skills she had built up over the years and explored ways of applying these in other situations and for other organisations. The consultants provided encouragement and helped to build her self-confidence. Importantly, they helped her to redefine herself as a freelance worker and to create her own 'company' structures. She is now self-employed and advises on the management of corporate identities. As a freelance worker she was able to make contacts through her old work colleagues as well as through friends in other areas of industry. She is able to generate a modest income from her work, but her weekly expenses, shared with her husband who is in full-time employment, are still subsidised by her redundancy package. This will continue while she builds up more clients. Dawn's working life is extremely inconsistent – she sometimes needs to work flat out for 24 hours on one project and then will have no work at all for a few days. Given the comparative disorder of her working life, she ensures other areas of her life are more structured – leisure time, holidays and social routines are all sacrosanct. 'It's as important to manage your time off work as well as on work,' she says. 'And you have to discipline yourself not to panic even when it looks as though you'll never have any work again.'

TRADITIONAL ARRANGEMENTS

To employers, academic institutions represent the most important source for new recruits. Every year thousands of newly qualified students enter the job market equipped with up-to-date skills and sound knowledge and anxious to make an impression on the outside world.

Over the past few years the proliferation of university degrees has led employers to take academic qualifications for granted. They are now more particular about their recruits and can even select candidates who are suited to the company's working culture and business priorities. There is competition between recruiters for candidates of the highest quality and new initiatives are being taken by employers to attract individual graduates to industries in which they may not have previously considered working.

Graduates need to find ways of standing out from the crowd. This can mean further study, vocational training or gaining particular skills and knowledge for that company. Some of these initiatives will follow graduation but developing your first job opportunity should begin while you are still an undergraduate.

While on your course there will be many opportunities to talk to and even work with professionals in your field of interest. Dissertations and research projects are a great excuse to phone up organisations and individuals you admire and to learn more about their work. Making the initial contact can be daunting, but in general people are flattered to find someone keen and interested in what they do and think. There may be a direct correlation between your college work and the activity of a company. Your own research may lead to improvements in a manufacturing process or to the development of a new product. A company may even express an interest in sponsoring you to research a subject relevant to their business. Interviewing a major employer or specialist on their pet subject can get your name known in the right circles and open doors for you in the future.

Similar relationships can be built through activities within the Students' Union. Excursions and presentations arranged by societies and clubs bring students into contact with professionals from all walks of life. The benefit from such a meeting may not immediately be obvious, but they are a good way to learn about the world of work.

The first specifically career-oriented contact you are likely to have with an employer will be at a careers fair. These are arranged by your college's Careers Service and may occur four or five times a year. Early on in the academic year the fairs will simply provide information about companies and the work they do. After Christmas similar fairs cover postgraduate study options but the main summer recruitment fairs take place in June and July.

Fairs often feature hundreds of employers from all sectors of industry and they can be overwhelming. You will be among thousands of students looking for work and unless you do some preparation before attending your visit may not be constructive. Think about the areas you want to find out about and if possible the individual companies you want to talk to. It is a good idea to take copies of your CV to give to potential employers. Other fairs are smaller and more specialised, addressing specific areas of work. Some organisations believe traditional fairs do not attract the right kind of recruit, or they may be too small to be noticed among the other exhibitors. One 'alternative careers fair' in Manchester covered work in the voluntary and charity sector.

Whatever the size or focus of the fair the principle is the same. Employers have stalls to provide information on working for their company. The stalls are run by experienced employees who will answer any questions you have. While there may be application forms, and even interview opportunities, at the fair, these events are useful simply to find out what kind of opportunities there are and which companies are recruiting.

Careers fairs are good for graduates but not very effective recruitment vehicles for businesses. They require experienced and skilled staff to run the stall and create presentation resources. The Association of Graduate Recruiters puts the annual cost of producing recruitment brochures for major companies at £5m; this expense may help to increase the company's profile but produce no suitable applicants. For this reason recruiters are becoming more strategic and focused in the way they target undergraduates.

Formal presentations reduce the amount of time and manpower required from the company and ensure students who attend have some prior interest in it. Arranged through the Careers Service or college departments, presentations give company representatives the chance to introduce the company to new recruits and answer specific questions.

One traditional method of recruitment is the Milk Round. A company visits a college or university and interviews suitable applicants over one or two days. The interviews can take place at any time from January through to the end of the academic year, depending on the industry and company, and applications are usually made two months earlier.

This form of recruitment is beginning to pick up again after many years of decline. The fall in graduate recruitment of the late 1980s meant companies could not justify the expense of sending staff around the country to interview candidates. This led to the perception that the process was a waste of time for students. Milk Round applications fell and many employers have since found it difficult to attract enough applicants to make a visit worthwhile in spite of an upturn in their recruitment. There has been an increase in Milk Round activity over the last few years, and improvements in the relationship between employers and the Careers Service mean this technique is regaining popularity.

Employers have realised that these forms of recruitment may not appeal to their ideal candidate. New technology has inspired new initiatives. ASDA supermarkets was one of the first organisations to use the Internet as part of their recruitment programme. This not only represents a new market-place for job seekers but also shapes the type of people the store attracts. There are now many employment resources on the Net including individual company home pages, CV databases and pages for workers with disabilities.

Some leading recruiters are employing head-hunting teams to seek out suitable undergraduates. This illustrates the competition that now exists between recruiters as well as the way in which employers will go out and find candidates rather than wait for them to approach the firm.

The new pattern of college recruitment reflects general changes in company organisation. In some cases recruitment has been decentralised, taken away from company headquarters and given

A fair way to apply

Michael Furrow was in the final year of an economics course when he first met representatives from an international steel manufacturing company at Manchester University's careers fair, and he did not have a firm idea of what he wanted to do after graduation. At the fair he met several companies interested in people with his qualifications, ranging from retail chain-stores to chartered accountants. Michael had a vague idea of the steel business, but had no idea what kind of employment this company could offer him. One of the people on their stand was David, who had graduated in economics three years previously. He was able to give Michael a detailed account of the work available in the organisation as well as the trainee programme for new recruits. David told Michael that the first few years in the company involved a lot of travelling as trainees tried out positions in different areas of the company. David himself had spent three months in the planning department in London followed by three months in one of the company's export depots on the coast. After their chat, Michael felt interested enough to leave his name and address with the representative and to take away information and the official application form. Having considered the material and all that had been said at the fair Michael applied for the traineeship. A few weeks later he was called for interview and was accepted on to the programme. 'I was very nervous about the fair because I thought they would decide whether to employ me there and then,' he says. 'If I hadn't stopped to talk I would not have realised the opportunities that were open to me. The information I took from the careers fair gave me the confidence to apply.'

over to individual departments and regional offices. This means that your application may be viewed by many different individuals and in various locations for the same company. It may also mean you can apply to different regional offices for work in the same organisation. Under the traditional pattern of recruitment students were employed in the summer of their graduation. Although this still occurs, many companies are moving towards year-round and 'just-in-time' recruitment. Economic fortune is not intertwined with the academic year and companies prefer to recruit when they need to rather than support superfluous graduates during slack periods. Year round recruitment means you should stay in touch with the careers centre to ensure you are aware of opportunities when they arise.

Your first step in employment may be to follow a graduate training scheme. These vary immensely from business to business but the basic idea is to integrate you into the company culture. For a small business this could simply mean being introduced to other members of staff and being shown how the office equipment works. Large national companies, on the other hand, run more complex courses, which describe the entire company structure and provide a number of learning experiences for graduates over the first 6–18 months.

If your employer has branches nationwide or worldwide you may find yourself moving around a great deal during your first years of employment. Working across a number of branches helps you understand how the company works and gives your employer a chance to see where you might fit in. This mobility can be very exciting but it also means that there is little chance of settling and putting down roots. Aware of this, some organisations make sure their graduates stay in one particular region where they can build up a base of friends. Others run support initiatives including social clubs and leisure activities where new graduates and employees can meet each other.

It is unlikely that you will finish studying when you begin work. While learning about the company you may need vocational or management qualifications. The cost of these will be met by your employer but finding the time and energy to study alongside full-time employment is extremely challenging.

Employing new graduates is a balancing act for recruiters. Graduates are keen to prove their worth to an employer and the employer naturally does not want to tarnish that enthusiasm. However, they can offer only a limited amount of responsibility since inexperience or naiveté may be detrimental to business. One retailer gives its graduates responsibility for an area of the shop floor for a limited number of weeks. This way recruits can have some impact on the working environment while still learning about the organisation.

Traineeships are constructive whether or not you decide to stay in that industry or with that company. They provide work experience and develop management and work skills relevant in other employment.

Working as part of a national or international company is extremely exciting. The scale of operation – managing large numbers of transactions, money, people or information – can satisfy the most ambitious of graduates. In addition, a large company has the resources to invest in, and develop, your talents, and may even provide a visible career path within the organisation.

Changes in company structure mean the career path is unlikely to be a simple progression from lower to middle and senior management. The economic pressures of the recession hit middle management positions in many organisations. 'Down-sizing' usually meant stripping out layers of management and reducing the payroll. Because there are fewer management positions, those who remain make quicker decisions, significantly increasing the speed of communications across the company.

However, there are two disadvantages to this. First, fewer management levels mean fewer promotion opportunities. Second, the promotions that do exist are steeper than before, with sudden increases in responsibilities that were previously split over two or three separate promotions. The result is that employees are waiting longer for promotion and experiencing difficulty in managing the promotions when they occur.

Many companies have flat management structures where the traditional hierarchy of responsibility and status has been replaced by teamwork and group responsibility. This structure has removed the traditional incentive of increased influence that employers offered their employees for hard work and longevity of service. Instead, all employees can get involved in the decision-making processes of the company. This restructure has also led to companies offering their workers other development resources, including education and careers advice, even facilitating development and learning experiences outside their own organisation.

Employees may mourn the loss of the traditional career ladder but it was not desirable from a company or individual's point of view. 'Stove-pipe ascendancy' meant an employee could rise to the board of directors having worked in only one department. A graduate entering the accounts department at junior level could work up through the ranks to head of department. At this level they would gain influence at board level despite understanding the business purely from their single discipline. Companies are now using 'carousel' development where managers are given experience in diverse departments throughout their ascent. This develops a more global view of the company and enables board members to make better informed decisions. 'Promotion' is, therefore, as likely to be sideways as it is to be upwards.

The proliferation of small- to medium-sized enterprises has offered graduates another challenging, if not so lucrative, opportunity for employment. Small independent companies are established in many areas of industry and have generated millions of new jobs. Although the scale of operation is smaller the advantage is that you are likely to have more involvement and influence over the entire workings of the company.

In a large company you will work in only one department at a time. You could be responsible for buying materials but have a limited knowledge of what happens when these materials arrive. In a small company you could find yourself buying the materials, arranging their delivery and storage and overseeing their application. Technology has helped here, allowing one person to manage many tasks. Desktop publishing packages, for example, have made magazine production a one- or two-person operation. A publication can be written, edited, laid out and even printed from one office. Teamwork is critical to the success of a small company. If you are working with only two or three others in one location then you must get on with these people in all events.

THE TRADITIONAL CAREER STRUCTURE

MEETING YOUR EMPLOYER

- Student's Union, society or club events
- undergraduate projects
- careers fairs, higher education fairs, alternative careers fair
- formal presentations

BEING RECRUITED

- application forms from careers fairs, presentations or direct requests to employers
- the Milk Round
- recruitment through company home-pages on the Internet
- head-hunting teams

GRADUATE TRAINEE PROGRAMMES

- introduction to company culture
- introduction to working life
- further vocational study and qualifications
- clear promotional path or career expectations

The combination of increased graduate numbers and fewer opportunities means that many graduates find themselves working in positions that do not require their level of skills or qualifications. This under-employment can be frustrating but is still a useful start to your career. You can use your talents and skills in any situation and, as the workplace changes, all jobs have enjoyed increases in responsibilities. It is still an opportunity to develop skills for the workplace, which is the first step to a good career. And if you convince your employer you are worth his investment by doing the job thoroughly and with enthusiasm who knows where it may lead?

THE PORTFOLIO CAREER

Over the past few years employment specialists have predicted the death of the job. This prediction is not based on levels of unemployment or on the lack of job security, but that the concept of being employed to do one particular task for one company over a long period of time is outdated. In his book *Jobshift*, William Bridges describes the job as an economic artefact; simply a way of allocating the work that needs to be done among the people who will do it. In today's fast moving business world this method of allocation is inflexible and inefficient.

Work was not always structured as it is today. Tradespeople used to be responsible for every aspect of their work. A blacksmith, for example, would be responsible for managing the operation of the forge as well as the satisfaction of each customer. The industrial revolution split production into separate components executed by dedicated workers. These workers then needed managers to co-ordinate their function with the other elements of production to ensure maximum efficiency. The boundaries between jobs were clear and well defined. There was no question as to where one person's responsibility stopped and another's started.

These boundaries do not exist in today's workplace. In a modern company there is an awareness that the work of one department directly affects the operation of another. Efficient manufacturing requires perfect communication between supply and production departments. In addition, the market-place is extremely volatile and companies need to be able to respond swiftly without being hampered by their own decision-making structures.

Another factor in this change has been the out-sourcing of some services. This trend started out in private organisations where cost savings were made by employing outside contractors rather than supporting an in-house department. These include areas such as marketing, recruitment and payroll services; areas that are expensive to run, have no direct impact on a company's turnover and may not be required all year round. The government has incorporated this business practice into the public sector with the result that local authorities now must put services out for competitive tender.

This has created new opportunities for suppliers. By identifying and meeting the specific demands of particular clients, suppliers can successfully operate in niche markets. With a large number of clients, companies can specialise and achieve economies of scale. A specialised service will be more satisfying for the customer than one from a general supplier.

Casualisation of employment has occurred throughout the workplace. It is more cost effective to employ staff as and when they are needed than to support them throughout the year regardless of the work load. Employment contracts are becoming short term and project based and sometimes do not exist at all. The psychological contract, a mutual understanding between employer and employee, has grown in importance and can replace written terms entirely. There may be no legal backing but it is in both parties' interest to create and maintain a good working relationship. Psychological contracts give both parties the flexibility to adapt to changes in business activities and to exploit other employment opportunities as they arise.

To gain some sense of unity and direction within this uncertain employment market, professionals and graduates must replace the idea of the traditional career with that of the portfolio career. This career plan recognises that you will have a large number of employers throughout your working life. Each piece of work you do adds to your portfolio of experience and skills. You may do similar work for each employer or you may do a wide variety of jobs in one particular industry. The wider your skills base, the wider the range of work available to you. Following a portfolio career is an accumulative process. Companies will want to employ candidates with the greatest experience so the greater the variety of your work, the greater the opportunities available to you.

The traditional career is function or industry based – a career in the army, a career as a television producer – and this can be extremely limiting. Your determination to work in one industry or one particular job may not be enough to conquer the competition for that position. If you base your career decisions on the skills you have and those you would like to develop, the area of your employment and your actual job become of secondary importance. The right work in any industry will satisfy your skill requirements. This approach extends the opportunities available to you while guaranteeing satisfying work.

Short-term contracts and project work are the fodder of the portfolio career. They are already common to some industries but are now spreading throughout the workplace. One of the best examples of this is film production. In order to make a film the production company will bring together a team of workers to carry out specific tasks. They will employ separate companies such as equipment hire or an outdoor catering service, as well as individual actors, designers and directors.

There is an incredible range of work to be done, but all those employed will work together, focused on the end product. Once the film is completed, or as each employee completes his or her work towards the film, the team splits up and moves on to their next project. Some may find work together, some may work in a completely different area. The catering company's next contract may be to provide food at a private function. The production company may decide to employ certain people again or the director may use certain staff again. Although the work has been short term, all those involved can advance their careers through the project, directly by using contacts made with other workers in the industry, or indirectly by increasing the experience and skills they have.

The construction industry is notorious for short-term casual contracts. Manual labourers have had to cope with temporary work for many years, but the same is true of the professional roles of site management, quantity surveying and even architectural work. Construction or maintenance projects may also involve many layers of subcontractors. The main contractor employed on design and building will contract out for earth movers, machinery and personnel. Complicated contractual arrangements can lead to confusion over who is responsible for each aspect of the project. This reinforces the need for good communication skills and teamwork in the workplace.

The length of each project will be different. You may carry out a task for one employer over many years while completing several shorter projects for other employers. Your individual role determines the length and security of your work. An architect is employed to design a building, whether or not it is actually built.

The manual labourer has to wait for the money and resources to become available. This is true of the role of film producer compared to that of the actor. The further down the line of command you are, the shorter your contract and the less certain your job. Professionals and graduates will be able to negotiate longer contracts since they are more likely to be in a management position. You may find that although you start at the bottom of your industry, as you work your way up you will gain more job security. The ability to work in more than one area of a project will also increase your job security. If you can assess the resources for a building and put that building up, a contractor is more likely to use you than they are to employ two separate companies.

The other important aspect of this arrangement is that your working relationships will vary from project to project. In one instance you may work directly for the client who is paying the bill while for another there may be several contractors or levels of management separating the two of you. Likewise you may be responsible for the entire final product, for one small aspect of the work or for managing other workers on the project. The project worker must be able to operate in a wide range of scenarios and be ready to take on the responsibilities each project brings.

Portfolio careers are not the prerogative of the self-employed freelance worker. You may find yourself in full-time employment for a company that provides a range of services for a number of clients. Business consultants work in many different areas of company operation, from recruitment to marketing. Information technology providers work in a wide variety of situations. While the business is the same, providing the client with the computer system best for them, the management of each project will vary according to that client's needs and organisation.

The main difference between following a traditional career or creating a portfolio career is whether you work for a single employer on a single function, or whether you work in many different roles for diverse employers and industries. The traditional career entails a change in employer or position every few years, securing new challenges, higher remuneration and responsibilities. The portfolio career is a conscious ongoing search for new opportunities and employers.

The first step of a portfolio career

English graduate Jane Seagrove always wanted to work in the media. She was not a performer but while at college she publicised Drama Society productions, securing reviews and previews in the local press. On one occasion she managed to get the local radio station to do a feature on a play that had been written by another student. She nurtured the initial contact and spent one summer working voluntarily for the radio station. Here she was able to build up contacts with more media-related organisations locally and nationally. She continued to help out at the radio station throughout her final year at college. When she graduated she took a part-time waiting job. Through her work at the radio station she discovered that the local theatre's press office was looking for an assistant. The theatre offered her a part-time contract, which meant she could leave her waiting job but maintain the relationship with the radio station. A few weeks later she was offered the chance to produce her own item for the radio arts programme. Her extensive contacts meant she was able to turn in a professional and engaging piece. She was paid for this article but, more importantly, now had professionally broadcast material to which she could refer when approaching other employers. 'The first year was difficult,' Seagrove admits, 'I didn't enjoy waiting at all but it was worth it for the experience I was able to get from the radio and theatre.' Two years out of university, Jane is keen to find new opportunities to work with radio and the theatre and to increase her skills in these areas. She is not worried about finding a full-time position: 'I enjoy the variety of working at both places,' she says. 'It's good to be able to keep your options open.'

In order to be able to find these challenges and provide consistently satisfying work, professionals must develop new skills in career management. Whether you are looking for long-term or portfolio-oriented employment, you cannot rely on an organisation to provide a career ladder or to coach you through your development. You must create your own career.

As a potential employee you offer unique skills. These are not purely academic but include your personality, interests and attitude. In order to gain employment you need to be aware of your strengths and promote these to employers. Alongside your actual money making activities you must market yourself, ensure your work is of a high standard and constantly update your skills to remain competitive.

Each individual professional is, in effect, a private company offering a unique service to an employer. It may seem impersonal to regard oneself as a business but, without an external company structure, promotion, training, remuneration and working conditions must all be set by you.

The portfolio career gives you the freedom to decide how to lead your life. You may be able to decide where you are going to work. Is the location determined by your current employer or will you need to locate your own offices or work from home? For how long will you work and what rewards will you give yourself? These are all decisions that previously your employer made for you and in some portfolio careers the decisions are still dictated by the area of work. Ultimately you make the choice of the area of work in which you want to operate and the circumstance in which that will take place. Deciding these things is not easy. Once made, following decisions and working for yourself require a great deal of dedication, self-belief and self-discipline.

As a nation we shy away from self-promotion, preferring to undersell ourselves to telling someone how good we are. This is a self-consciousness that workers can ill afford. Competition and value for money in the market-place mean that if you cannot demonstrate the benefits your employment will bring to an organisation, you will not be employed. There is also a great deal of cynicism attached to success through networking. 'The old-boys network' suggests employees gain work because of who they know rather than on merit. It is understandable that jobs are filled because someone knows someone; if you were embarking on a business venture would you take on a complete unknown who had the right qualifications or someone who was recommended, who you knew could do the job and who you got on well with?

A successful portfolio career depends on creating a good network of contacts throughout your world of work. Careers, job centres and advertisements are only the tip of the iceberg of opportunities to work. Speculative inquiries to companies or CVs with covering letters hitting the right desk at the right time can pay off in the long run. Even if you find yourself filed away 'for future reference' your interest in the company will be noted and your name will be known.

The easiest way to network is through family and friends. This does not necessarily mean getting a job because your uncle owns the company but you may know someone already in the industry who can give you useful advice and information. They may know of a new company setting up, or be able to explain future developments to you. Social gatherings within the industry, such as presentations and launch parties, are the ideal opportunity for making influential friends, promoting yourself and keeping up to date with developments. Friends from college may also work in your industry. You may be able to help each other find opportunities or team up and offer companies your combined skills.

Work experience is the gateway to a strong network. It provides a foot in the door and introduces you to the working culture of an organisation. While at work you may meet other people who can offer you employment opportunities. You should use this time to find out as much as you can about the industry in which you are working. Obviously you must be careful not to pester potential employers too much, but showing an interest in company activities can be as fruitful as being a reliable and efficient worker.

A common experience of many graduates on leaving college is under-employment. You may find yourself working in a situation which does not fully utilise your skills. During school or summer vacations you may have taken shop or bar work to earn some money for holidays or to support yourself in college. After graduation this could be the only kind of work available to you.

Under-employment is frustrating for you and difficult for relatives to understand, especially if they expected your education to enable you to walk straight into a good job. However, there can be a number of benefits. At least you have an easy, albeit paltry, income while you decide what your next step will be. Doing a task that is in no way related to your area of study will enable you to step back from the years of education and take an objective viewpoint. You can clarify your next move rather than dashing after the first opportunity to show itself. You may want to raise cash quickly to go travelling, to invest in further education or to buy equipment for your desired area of work. Under-employment in your chosen industry is excellent work experience and enables you to see how the business operates from the inside.

Trade journals exist for practically every area of industry. Apart from carrying specific job advertisements they will contain valuable information about companies and market trends. You may read about a company that has recently won a new contract or is on the verge of expansion and a well-worded letter to the managing director explaining how you want to contribute to his company's success will show you are serious about the industry.

The portfolio career gives you complete control over the direction of your career. You can concentrate on one area of work if you wish, or consciously diversify across many industries. Portfolio careers are likely to bring you into contact with a wider range of people and experiences than traditional careers. Working for yourself can be stressful and building up working contacts early in your career can be frustrating, but taking control of your career means you will not be side-tracked into an occupation you do not like or find yourself stuck in a dead-end job without the skills to move on. At the end of the day, it is probably a less stressful arrangement than being at the beck and call of a single employer who makes inconvenient demands or can make you redundant at a moment's notice.

THE PORTFOLIO CAREER

WHY?

- lack of job security
- lack of job boundaries
- out-sourcing services
- short-term or project based contracts

WHAT IS IT?

- many employers, many jobs
- skills-based employment
- temporary team work
- self-employment and freelance work

THE KEY TO STARTING A PORTFOLIO CAREER

- develop a network of workplace contacts
- identify work suitable for your skills
- self-promotion
- gain work experience

THE LONG VIEW

The workplace has always been in constant change but today the changes are faster and more radical. Cradle-to-grave employment is no longer feasible, as no single employer can guarantee long-term remuneration or a career ladder with increasing responsibilities. It is impossible to tell which industries or companies will succeed and which will be superseded, bought out or closed down from week to week. Employees have suffered financially and health-wise from job insecurity. But while older workers have had to adapt to these changes you will be part of the first generation to face them from your first day at work. It is not simply your working life that will be different from that of your parents, or even of people 5–10 years older than you; it could be your entire lifestyle.

There is some resistance to the idea that full-time traditional employment is a thing of the past. Understandably those with full-time traditional jobs are unlikely to accept that there is change until their own positions are affected. The perception of change is also obscured because the job market is currently at a point of transition. Traditional jobs are declining but do still exist. More importantly, tax, welfare and other support structures are geared towards the traditional job rather than short-term project work. Workers on short-term contracts today particularly suffer because society and the government have a fixed idea of what constitutes full-time employment.

Historically, work has been the central axis to life. The job provides financial security and supports mortgages, holidays and day-to-day family life. We spend most of our lives working, earning income to spend on leisure activities. Work also provides personal identity, status, friends and colleagues. One need only look at how the closure of the coal mines destroyed entire communities to understand the far-reaching affects of changes in work culture. Changing how people are employed will have an immense impact. Take away the job and not only do financial commitments become more difficult to manage, but we lose a vital source of social engagement.

It has always been assumed that each generation of workers builds on the success of the previous generation. Their achievements are ultimately greater, their rewards higher and their lifestyle more luxurious. This is no longer a certainty. Stripping out levels of management has reduced the number of financially rewarding positions available to the next generation of workers. Advancement is also difficult to achieve when financial pressures mean senior executives are inclined to retain their positions rather than let new talent through.

Graduate salaries are still competitive and maintain an advantage over non-graduate wages but the reduced promotional ladder means professionals can look forward to a slower rise in remuneration and, in some cases, less disposable income compared to workers of a few years ago. With no guaranteed future income it is difficult to buy a house, support a family or even find a credit card company that will trust you. Full-time employment can require a high level of geographical mobility for moving between employers or within single organisations. As a result professionals are unable to settle down until later in life.

Jobs that have not disappeared have expanded, involving more responsibilities, increasing the pressure on employees and taking more of their time. Work completely dominates some people's lives and stress is a serious issue for many organisations. A new problem of 'presenteeism' has emerged among some employees who work obsessively for long hours in order to justify their employment. Such activity is clearly unhealthy and can lead to substandard work, increased absence and reduced productivity.

There has always been a thin line between doing a highly paid but stressful and demanding job and working so hard that you cannot enjoy the rewards work brings you. Now that companies cannot compensate difficult working environments with high incomes the emphasis has moved towards providing job satisfaction and an enjoyable working culture. The job is losing its central function of providing the means to live the rest of your life and becoming recognised as an important independent aspect of life. This can be seen in attitudes among recent graduates and in corporate human resources departments.

Graduates are seeking jobs that provide a high level of satisfaction rather than remuneration. The social role of work has increased in importance. Community and environmental work is very popular and many graduates work for voluntary groups. Small- and medium-sized enterprises offer a far more informal working structure than that of the multinationals. Although they cannot offer the same scale of activity they can offer graduates a wide range of satisfying opportunities. More and more graduates are setting up their own businesses, creating the opportunity to do precisely what they want to do.

Previously concerned with staff welfare and hiring and firing, personnel and human resource departments of large organisations are now looking at ways to motivate and develop their staff. Initiatives such as 'Investors in People' demonstrate a company's commitment to employees. Organisations are concerned to foster a sense of community among the workforce and create some degree of continuity in the face of the fragmented workplace.

Some graduates and professionals are enjoying lucrative careers through temporary work. There are many agencies and employment consultants who are in effect providing full-time work for skilled people. This trend will continue in the future to the point where agencies can offer their employees corporate benefits previously afforded by the larger employers.

It has been suggested that society in the future will be split between those who have the right skills in order to work and those whom the job market will simply leave behind. For some workers this is already the case. The process is already happening and a vicious dichotomy is emerging where one section of the workforce suffers because they have too much work to do while the other section is left on the shelf.

As short-term project-related work proliferates throughout commerce and industry the pattern of working life will become disjointed. Rather than entering a career aged 21 and steadily working through the industry for 40 years, workers may have short periods of work and then be unemployed before the next contract comes along. Workers will follow a cycle of activity and unemployment throughout their career. At the moment people are scared of being out of work and a CV with patches of unemployment appears unattractive to an employer used to seeing a constant linear progression in a candidate's experience. In the future the concept of unemployment could alter. As long as time spent away

Portrait of a future worker

Harry Trentam is married with two children and owns his own home. He graduated twenty years ago with a degree in geography. He has never been employed by a single employer for more than two years. His CV shows he has worked for many different employers ranging from evening work for a market research company to project work for a design-and-build construction company. He is currently working as a business consultant for companies setting up international ventures. He has been without work on 5 occasions since graduating, the longest period of which was 14 months. He used this time to gain language skills, which enabled him to secure his next job. His work is the result of many years' experience in a variety of business scenarios. He works abroad for up to 8 weeks at a time but then spends at least one month at home with his family. His knowledge is extensive and wide-ranging and his skills are unique so clients are willing to pay him well for his services. Whereas today he easily makes enough money to cover costs of family life, he needed support through his early career from a finance company who were sensitive to his position. They understood his working arrangements and gave him credit and a number of specially designed financial products, which ensured he could access a steady income throughout the year. His pension scheme, for example, began fifteen years ago and allows him to vary his payments throughout the year depending on how much money he can afford to contribute each month. Harry gets a lot of satisfaction from dealing with a wide variety of clients and in the future he hopes to set up his own advisory office, which will provide consultancy services in some of the countries he works in. He knows this will not happen until his family have grown up. He also knows that he will need additional skills, support and guaranteed clients if the project is to succeed and he will work to secure all three over the next decade.

from direct employment is not completely wasted it could become an acceptable part of the job cycle and no longer stigmatised as is currently the case. Few people expect to retire aged 60 or 65 and take no further part in economic activity. In the future the welfare state will not be able to cope with the ageing population. Retirement is becoming too expensive. The pension does not support a satisfactory lifestyle and consequently employees continue to work into their old age. Perhaps the new job cycle will be a continual movement between states of work and retirement.

Short-term contracts mean companies are not obliged to provide any benefits, pensions, sick pay or holidays. However, the best employers will recognise the motivation and commitment benefits of providing this support to all employees regardless of their contract. Pensions, private medical insurance, insurance against loss of earnings and repossession will be the responsibility of individuals but the complete package of benefits is currently far too expensive for most people. Companies have greater buying power and so should be able to offer employees access to such schemes.

As new working structures establish themselves, new financial products, tax and benefit systems will evolve. The move towards self-assessment of income tax in part recognises that PAYE is not the best way of taxing the workforce. The job-seekers allowance, on the other hand, still presumes that there is a full-time job waiting for every unemployed individual. In the future, financial support will need to facilitate an individual's move between diverse employment situations with the minimum of disruption to other areas of their lives.

It is impossible to pin down exactly what the new working structures might mean. Full realisation is some way off and whether the job market ever achieves stability is open to question. What is important is to bear these possibilities in mind when entering the workplace. Single-minded pursuit of the nine-to-five job is unwise, partly because that job may not exist, but mainly because that way of work is inflexible to any future changes.

Competition in the market-place has given rise to the idea that if you have a job you should stick to it. You are lucky to have that job and there are plenty of other people who are ready and willing

THE LONG VIEW

WHAT WILL GO

- long-term, single employer work
- financial security
- reliable promotion ladder

WHAT WILL COME

- informal and short-term work for many employers
- cyclical employment and inactivity
- new commercial and governmental support initiatives for short-term workers

OLD ASSUMPTIONS	NEW THINKING
• there is a full-time job for everyone	• there are infinite opportunities for work
• if you have a job, stick with it	• always seek out satisfying employment
• go for the job you want	• create the career and home life you want

to do it, usually for less money. This is neither a true nor a useful view. Firstly, if you were employed on the basis of your skills then it is unlikely that there is anyone else out there who can do the job as well as you can. Second, this attitude provides no help if you are under-employed or if you decide you do not like your job. If you keep yourself informed of the job market and keep your skills up-to-date you can take control of your career and take employment for positive reasons, such as learning new skills and gaining new experiences, rather than negative ones.

The fluid nature of the workplace has led the Association of Graduate Recruiters to advise students to start thinking about their career from as early an age as possible. Given the lack of career structure, students need to focus on where they want to go and ensure that the academic subjects they follow are relevant. Forward planning also enables them to gain the experience and skills they need for work from higher education. This will enable them to enter their chosen profession with the necessary qualifications and attitudes to succeed. But this degree of forward planning is depressing since it is a move away from enjoying diverse experiences or allowing the unpredictable to influence your career. The approach also does nothing for graduates and professionals already seeking work whose education was not so career-oriented.

The main principle, however, is applicable. Since there are few career structures, and the ones that do exist do not provide long-term security, you must determine your own direction. Fluctuations in the market-place are strong enough to side-track you into areas in which you do not wish to work. It is too easy to take a job because it's there and then build up financial commitments that mean you cannot leave that job.

Determining your career is not so much considering a job as considering your lifestyle. In the short term you may want to pay off the bank loan while in the long term you want to work with children. In the short term you may want to work in a specific industry and in the long term you will work in order to support a family. These priorities should determine how you work as much as the employment opportunities available. There is nothing wrong with working simply in order to finance the house, car and holiday, nor with living on the poverty line but doing something in which you passionately believe. You must determine for yourself the balance between 'work' and 'life' activities. If you are clear about these then whatever you do will fit into your career and lead you in the right direction.

THE SKILLS YOU WILL NEED

SKILLS FOR THE WORKPLACE

Skills for the workplace are a blend of industry-specific knowledge and work-related, 'transferable skills'. You may gain the former through academic study and your own personal interest. The latter skills can be more difficult to obtain. They depend on work experience either within the industry or in a comparable position of responsibility. Work experience of any kind is a great opportunity to learn about the working culture and priorities of an industry from the inside. This kind of knowledge will convince future employers that you understand the business and can contribute to the direction of their company.

Higher education qualifications attract higher starting salaries. Recent surveys of graduate vacancies and salaries show employers experiencing a shortfall in recruitment among scientific, technical, engineering and research and development staff so degrees in scientific subjects are in great demand. The demand reaches into the education sector where special incentives are available to trainee teachers of science. However, the Association of Graduate Recruiters describes a degree as 'the benchmark of intellectual competency'. A qualification is proof that an individual has attained a certain level of academic proficiency, no more and no less. It does not entitle the holder to full time employment nor does it suggest the graduate is fit for the workplace. As the number of degree holders rises graduates cannot even rely on higher education to make them stand out from the crowd.

Some degree courses are vocational, such as medical and architectural qualifications. However, viewing all qualifications, further and research degrees included, as simply a mark of intellectual achievement means you have complete freedom of choice for your career. This is particularly important when you consider that 40 per cent of new opportunities are open to graduates of any discipline.

Companies are keen to avoid employing and paying a recruit who will take six months of training and developing before contributing to the bottom line of the company. Graduates who have already proven their capabilities in a work situation will be in a better position to secure employment. They have transferable skills; skills that are useful in many, if not all, work environments rather than being company or activity specific.

Business awareness and communication skills have always been high on the agenda for employers looking for new recruits. Other skills include time management, self-motivation and commitment. These skills lie at the heart of most jobs. You can easily pick up company-related knowledge, work processes, procedures and so on, but this knowledge will be pointless if you cannot use it constructively. The ability to learn is also an extremely important skill for any employer as it shows you will be able to take on new ideas and concepts rather than assuming you know it all. If a company is to adapt to the constant changes in the market-place its staff should be ready to take on new practices and develop their working techniques. The ability to learn is one transferable skill that your degree clearly proves you have.

Communication, team-working and leadership skills are also highly prized in the job market especially as work becomes more team oriented. These are skills that you will have used at college in project work, seminars, tutorials and presentations. You may have organised events, attended debates or been involved in the running of the Students' Union. All of these activities required effective communication on your part. Such skills come more naturally to some people than to others and the Careers Service will be able to suggest workshops where they can be acquired and developed. Equally you can set yourself tasks or put yourself in a position where you have to use these skills; liaising with other people, negotiating arrangements and motivating people. All these are fundamental skills required for managing a group of employees or securing a deal with a client.

Scanning job advertisements in newspapers or at careers and job centres will give you a clear idea of the kind of person employers are seeking. Adverts include descriptions such as 'team-worker', 'self-starter' and 'juggler', all of which refer to the way in which you work rather than the task you work on. Some even specify personal characteristics such as a good sense of humour, determination, confidence and the ability to stay calm.

Employers know they will be able to recruit someone with the right qualifications so they want to make sure that person is suited to their workplace and will get on with other employees. You may believe yourself to be the right kind of person for that task but you must be able to offer clear evidence of this. Never pretend you fit an employer's work culture as you will be unhappy there and your employment will probably be short-lived.

All graduates, regardless of industry or activity, must be conversant with information technology. If you have managed to get through life so far without knowing what a mouse is or how Windows works, go and sign up for a course immediately. Computers are used extensively throughout the workplace, from retail to restoration work, product design to personnel management. If you take a management position you will probably wordprocess your own correspondence. If you are in purchasing or stock control you will use barcodes to update information.

Some industries rely on IT more than others, and knowledge of particular software and hardware can give you a head start. Working in the publishing industry usually requires experience with AppleMac computers and the QuarkXpress program. Technology is constantly finding new applications in the workplace and affecting business in diverse ways. The Internet offers a global marketplace for company products as well as a cheap and effective way of finding staff. Search programs and CV databases make the Internet the ideal way for companies to find suitable workers globally. Awareness of what technology can do will enable you to help your employer expand their business and may even help you find your employer.

Whatever job you apply for and whatever company you approach, your CV and letter of application should be wordprocessed and tailored for that company's particular requirements. You could pay private rates and hope other people will present your skills in the best way but it is just as easy to gain access to the wordprocessing facilities through friends or college. Furthermore, it's a great opportunity for you to demonstrate your own technical abilities.

THE SKILLS YOU WILL NEED FOR THE WORKPLACE

TRANSFERABLE SKILLS

- oral and written communication
- teamwork
- initiative
- leadership
- time management and organisation
- enthusiasm
- business acumen
- interpersonal skills
- motivation
- computer literacy

WHERE TO DEVELOP SKILLS

- managing academic and social commitments at college
- involvement in society and club activities
- work experience in any capacity
- short-term training courses, personal and business training exercises
- industry and academic run workshops

SKILLS FOR YOU

Until graduation most of the objectives you work towards are set out for you. Throughout your education there are pre-set targets for course work and examinations. With graduation an infinite number of possibilities are open to you and in theory you are now fully equipped to take your place in future employment.

After completing a degree course it can be hard to decide what to do for the next few weeks, let alone years. The absence of job security or a well defined career path means it is up to you to provide a course of action. This course may be to find a steady job, accept the associated discipline and enjoy the geographical, financial and social stability it brings. But the job you take may not last for long or you may decide it is not for you. Unless you have identified your long-term goals you will find it difficult to change your circumstances and move in a constructive direction.

Some experts believe the majority of graduates 'fall into' their work as a result of chance or whim rather than any positive decision. Given the unpredictability of the job market this is not surprising. If you have a good network of friends and contacts it is likely that chance will get you more work than any number of application forms. A conversation or passing remark could hold the key to major opportunities. If you remain focused on what your long term aims are, even if you fall into a job you do not particularly like you can still exploit the situation for the rewards and experience it offers.

At this point there is a temptation to follow the cue of many other career and life management manuals, assume an evangelical tone and talk about self-belief and the importance of a positive mental attitude to success. (Believe in your abilities, believe in your desires, think positively and you will get positive results.) Rather than addressing positive thinking as a New Age faith, it is more appropriate to view it as a separate skill; the skill of being a self-starter.

Many employers want self-starters in their companies. These are people who can come up with bright ideas, new initiatives and follow them through with little help from those around them. In creating your own career you must be a self-starter, taking the initiative and exploiting the opportunities that appear to you and that will take you in the direction you want to go. Self-employed people create their own opportunities, establishing their own shops or marketing their services; things that simply would not happen unless they made them happen.

You need to be positive about what you are doing but base this on actual achievements rather then trying to generate a positive attitude regardless of circumstances. To do this you need to define your own success criteria. You set your own tasks and deadlines and reward yourself when you achieve them. These tasks may even form part of your search for work. Your aim for one week may be to fill out an application form or research a prospective employer.

Your success is usually recognised by those around you – your tutor, family or friends – rather than yourself. Although getting a highly paid job, promotion or turning in good work is self-satisfying it is not the same if other people do not acknowledge the achievement. You must learn to appraise your own performance and recognise your own accomplishments. Your successes will be appreciated by other people but they may not conform to other people's expectations. Your own assessment is therefore extremely important.

Measuring success effectively requires knowledge of current practice within your industry. You may gain this awareness through your own network of contacts in the industry, but there are also a number of formal networks you can key into, such as professional industry bodies, societies, associations or trade unions. Such organisations will keep you in touch with innovations in the workplace and provide information on new opportunities. A constant and varied base of contacts, whether friends, fellow workers or officials, will provide an invaluable source of support for your work and the social context traditionally afforded through workplace colleagues. The rise in teleworking and self-employment has inspired networks for home-workers that give information and support for those workers regardless of their business. Sharing work experience and even unemployment experience will help you to cope with continuing change and uncertainty in the workplace.

Staying in one job through fear that someone is waiting to take your place can be detrimental to your own personal development.

Stagnating in one company is effectively 'de-skilling'. Your talents and outlook could be rendered obsolete by the changing workplace outside. You may be very successful at your job but if that job were to disappear would you be able to work for any other company? Even if you have job security you should regularly assess your skills base and consider whether you need to move on and find new challenges.

Few employers offer fulfilling and challenging work over a number of years. Graduates who are under-employed in jobs that do not require a degree are not in a position to be recognised or developed. Small- and medium-sized companies may not be big enough to offer any promotional opportunities. If you are employed in response to a short-term need, once the need has gone your job will go. Your next job may not bring an increase in remuneration or even in responsibilities but it will always bring new opportunities and challenges. It will give you the chance to work in a different way and so continue to develop your skills.

The new skills required by graduates in the job market have been described by the Association of Graduate Recruiters as self-reliance skills. These are career management and learning skills through which individuals take responsibility for their own development. Self-awareness is the key to effective career management. Knowing your strengths will enable you to promote yourself effectively and work to the best of your abilities. Knowing your weaknesses will help you avoid positions that do not suit your working style and to identify those skills you should develop.

You have already used some of these skills in managing your study at college. As student numbers have increased, the ratio of students to tutors has increased and personal tutor time decreased. You have had to take more responsibility for your own study than previous generations. You will have decided independently on your specialist areas of study and motivated yourself to complete projects rather than waiting for tutors to penalise lethargy. If you consider the amount of work you did at college, the academic subjects you researched and the number of social and extra-curricula activities you took part in, you will realise that you already have time management skills and self-motivation skills.

The concept of 'lifelong learning' is also important. This is the idea that no worker ever reaches the end of his or her learning curve. Since the workplace is in constant change, workers need to constantly learn new skills and update their attitude to work. Life-long learning can mean taking official training courses, private non-vocational courses and learning from activities in the workplace. It benefits you as an individual, pushing your career forwards and stimulating your interest while your employer benefits from a workforce with increasing skills and knowledge. Information technology and the Internet are prime examples of where lifelong learning is being used. Workers of all ages have learnt how to use technology at work and realise they will continue to learn new skills as the technology evolves. Companies with sufficient resources promote learning throughout their organisation with in-house courses, employee education sponsorships and other initiatives. For the self-employed, funding education can be a problem especially if it requires investment in equipment.

The ability to learn is the most important skill you need to secure work and it was this skill that enabled you to gain your qualifications. It will now help you move between companies and industries and apply your skills to new situations. It will help you to be innovative in your approach to work and identify new opportunities to work. Maintaining an inquisitive mind and improving your own knowledge and skills are essential if you want employers to regard you as a worthwhile investment.

SUMMARY

SELF-RELIANCE SKILLS

- **self-awareness** – knowing your strengths and weaknesses and the best ways in which you work
- **self-promotion** – marketing your skills to an employer
- **exploring and creating opportunities** – finding employment and experiences to match your career aims
- **action planning** – deciding a course of action and sticking to it
- **networking** – generating and using good contacts within your area of work
- **negotiation** – getting the best out of your opportunities
- **political awareness** – an understanding of how large organisations work and the ability to fit into that culture
- **coping with uncertainty** – managing changes in life and work style
- **a development focus** – continually developing skills throughout life, both practically and in the classroom
- **transfering skills** – applying skills and knowledge across different industries and disciplines
- **self-confidence** – believing in your abilities and in the contribution you can make to an organisation.

PART TWO

THE WORKPLACE AND THE WORK

THE WORKPLACE

Your job does not necessarily determine the location or environment in which you will work. Clearly if you take up medicine or construction work you are unlikely to practise from an office block but you could design a product, work on statistics or write reports anywhere. Laptop computers, fax modems and mobile phones mean you can even do this while travelling. The place where you go to work each day is crucial to your enjoyment of work and the rest of your life. Banking work may inspire you but commuting to work every day or sitting behind a desk in an open plan office could make your life a misery. In the same way that assessing your skills helps to identify work suitable for you, considering where you want to work can also generate useful ideas.

Work experience will already have given you a feel for certain working conditions. A position as Saturday shop assistant may have put you off the idea of any customer-facing work. Academic work will have provided experience of working independently and as part of a team. You will know your best methods of working and which bring you the greatest satisfaction. Do you enjoy making the final product or contributing to an ongoing process? Do you get satisfaction out of contributing to the team or by completing something on your own? How much external guidance do you need in order to get things done? The answers to these questions will indicate whether you will be happiest working among a group of people or independently. They will also help you decide whether you

43

can operate in a high pressure, crowded working environment or in silence and solitude.

The speed at which you work is another important consideration. Some people put off work until the last minute and still produce excellent results overnight. Others need more time to consider and develop ideas. The speed of work and related stress levels differ from industry to industry. The demand for your product or service will also affect the way you work. Food retail managers tend to work in larger stores, with more stock lines, a faster turnover and more staff than hardware or household furnishing retailers.

What do you want to work with? You may want to work with other people but do you want to work with them as clients, customers or colleagues? You may prefer dealing with facts and figures, analysing and assessing data in order to provide advice. You may have practical or manual skills, which you can use working with raw materials in order to create a product. This could be anything from renovation work to sculpting to writing music. If you are uncertain what kind of job you want, finding a position that addresses these criteria could be the key to finding satisfactory employment.

Most graduate opportunities in business and management are office-based jobs. The office environment has changed in recent years in personnel structure, equipment and design of the workspace. These changes are the result of the globalisation of business and the need to cut costs.

Information, money, people and other resources can move around the world quickly and efficiently on a large scale. A company may have its most lucrative market on the other side of the world. A business is in direct competition with every similar practitioner worldwide as well as every other UK company. Maintaining that competitive edge has resulted in cost-cutting and bureaucracy-reducing initiatives such as the virtual office and just-in-time production lines.

The 'virtual office' staffed by 'tele-commuters' is another product of information technology. Affordable technology has enabled employees to work on home computers and receive faxes and information from their place of work via phone lines and e-mail. Some employees work from home on a regular basis since this offers a refreshing variety of workplace, fewer distractions and enables them to fit work around family life. In addition, the employee avoids a time wasting and frustrating journey to work.

One UK computer consultancy halved the resources it needed at their head office by making all their employees mobile tele-commuters. The workers were system trouble-shooters and oper-ated on-site in their client's premises. Each consultant was given a laptop, a car phone and fax machine enabling them to move directly between clients and keep in touch with head office without having to physically return there at any point in the day. Head office, although half its original size, was still effective as a 'drop-in' resource centre for the workers. The consultants found the style of working much more enjoyable. They could decide when to work and arrange their day around personal commitments. While the move cut costs by saving time and operating costs the greatest finan-cial gain came through an increase in productivity.

Chiat Day, an advertising agency in the US, completely destroyed their traditional office space. They removed all designated personal offices and threw the space open for employees to use as they wished. On arrival, each employee picks up a laptop computer and mobile phone, both of which can be connected to the office com-munication system anywhere in the building. Removing designated areas was intended to break down the formal barriers offices can create. This new freedom would carry over into the workforce's atti-tude and the work they created.

It is not possible to physically restructure every workplace but the move towards flatter management structures and more team-work is very popular. Just-in-time production carries many savings for storage and wasted stock by providing the raw materials and labour to meet a specific demand. Managing a process to these deadlines requires excellent communication skills and shared pri-orities between professional and manual staff. Barriers between employee hierarchies are being broken down so everyone can con-tribute to all areas of the company. ASDA and Rover Cars have engendered this idea into their culture by referring to all staff as 'Associates' rather than by their hierarchical position.

Abandoning company hierarchy leaves each employee free to operate in different teams from project to project. The computer consultancy Logica employs staff in one of nine company divisions

A new factory structure

Craven Lighting's manufacturing plant was restructured two years ago in order to integrate a number of cost-cutting strategies. The company employ about 1000 manual workers, 14 on-site designers and a general management staff of six. The company had long been at the mercy of the market and staff were laid off and re-employed almost every six months according to the fluctuating demand. This uncertainty had a demoralising effect on the entire workforce. Under the new structures the company guaranteed job security to all its workers on the understanding that they would work in any part of the company as and when required. If orders were down, a machine operator would willingly help in the testing department, or if he had completed an order he would help packing and dispatch. The workforce were arranged in teams to complete each job and encouraged to make suggestions on improving production efficiency through a bonus scheme. The factory operated on a 'just-in-time' basis, so raw materials arrived at the precise moment production needed them and completed orders were immediately loaded and sent out to the customer. This move cut down the amount of space taken up in storage and the number of man-hours required to oversee warehouse procedures. The new practice meant management had to adopt new initiatives. They were no longer simply sole managers for their section and were able to influence the work of other departments. They set up consultation sessions, which increased communications between themselves and the workforce. The previous hierarchy was replaced by a culture of teamwork, and competition existing between departments was replaced by joint responsibility. Some management staff left the company, unable to adapt to this new culture. Those who remained were keener to work together for the company's success.

but there is little hierarchy within the department and each employee works according to their skills and the project's demands. There is no unique place of work. If a consultant is needed in a different part of the country or world the company supports them in that place. While it may appear Logica staff move casually from one project to another, there is a complex personnel management system backed up by excellent cross-company communications ensuring the right people get the right opportunities. Staff are responsible for their own development but facilitating this flexibility is a constant investment for the company.

Like many other companies, Logica realises the importance of ensuring staff feel valued and that they belong. While some employees enjoy the lack of hierarchy and the constant geographical and social movement from project to project the lifestyle can be alienating. An extensive employee support culture offers many social and leisure activities throughout the company. Logica even employ a full time member of staff to organise such events. Graduate trainees at W H Smith are part of a trainee network, enabling them to share problems and gain support from each other, even though they may be geographically distant from one another.

Companies are becoming aware of the social responsibility they have towards their workforce. While it is too early, and hopeful, to herald the employee-centric company, creating a contented and highly motivated workforce has clear economic benefits. Formal schemes such as health care plans, share ownership and performance-related pay are intended to bind employee interests to the long-term interests of the company. They are both attempts to gain the commitment of the employee and to make the priorities of the company their own priorities.

Some office cultures will suit you more than others. Your work style may depend upon a visible company structure to establish what you are responsible for, who you report to and where your next promotion lies. Alternatively you may find such structures stifling. Dealing with authority and delegating tasks can be stressful but teamwork can be stressful too and attempts to flatten hierarchies, making all employees equal can be condescending. If flat management structures are to increase communications and achieve efficiencies they demand a good deal of compromise and tact. If you are used to making your own decisions and acting upon them you may be frustrated working by consensus.

Self-employment is increasing in all areas of business. Consultants, accountants, artists, craft and technical workers are all finding more opportunities freelancing than with one single employer. Working for yourself requires additional resources and one of these is a location from which you can work.

It may be that the service you provide occurs on-site with the client. A business consultant will visit a factory in order to assess processes and return to give the client advice. A computer consultant will work on-site with the client's equipment. If you are involved in manual work you may need workshop or storage space. Whatever you do there are always paperwork and phone calls, and other administration requiring a separate office or that must be done from home.

Integrating home life with work is a challenge. Office politics may be irritating and frustrating but at least you are able to leave work at work and come home to relax. Balancing work and home life requires a great deal of self-discipline. Without the presence or expectations of an employer will you be able to ignore the television or stop yourself from making another cup of coffee rather than working? If you are co-habiting will you be able to work undisturbed and use the phone without inconveniencing other people? Working at home can put pressures on relationships. You may find it difficult if you have a young family demanding your attention. There is also the danger of never being able to get away from work. Every time you relax your accounts are calling to you from the other room.

On the other hand you may be able to coordinate work and leisure activities in an efficient way. If you manage self-employment effectively you need not stick to office hours. You can avoid the boredom of being tied to the desk during slack periods and reward yourself with time off when you most appreciate it. Some home-workers create daily routines similar to those of conventional jobs. They set specific working hours, take no social calls during the day, conscientiously dress for work and even mimic the journey to work by going for a walk before starting.

There is more to considering the workplace than simply whether you are outside during the day or in an office. How work is done is far more influential than where it is done. When considering your job you should not think purely about the task you want to do but how you want to work. What kind of hours do you want? How much stress and responsibility can you happily cope with? Do you want to work with large numbers of people or work alone? Whatever work you take on you need to ensure it either supplies or supports a satisfying lifestyle outside working hours. The balance is up to you. You may be happy to work all hours for great financial remuneration, you may take a boring nine-to-five job to support a great social life. Alternatively you may find the work you do so much fun and so exciting the rest of you life is immaterial.

SUMMARY

WHERE WILL YOU WORK?

- producing a final product or contributing to a process
- in a team or on your own
- with high pressure or at a relaxed pace
- with clients, customers, colleagues, facts, figures, raw materials
- in a fixed or flexible structure
- self-employed, in a company or within an informal network
- at home or in a discreet location
- fixed hours or as many as needed

THE WORK

Work can be split into two types of activity; manufacturing a product or providing a service. It is difficult to divide all jobs in this way. Sculptors and singer-songwriters will strongly resist the idea that they are manufacturing a product. Equally a line manager responsible for a team of workers building cars may not regard his activity as a service. Identifying exactly what the job does is important, as the two activities have different priorities and one is likely to prove more satisfying for you than the other. Deciding whether you are a service provider or manufacturing a product will help you effectively promote and use your skills with an employer.

Manufacturing entails creating a product that can be sold on to a customer. Successful manufacturing depends on the popularity of your product. You can fulfil an existing demand or create a new market. The difference between what it cost you to make and what your customers will spend on it brings financial success. This requires a sound knowledge of your customers and efficient production processes. You must be highly motivated to produce your product and have faith that people will buy it. Manufacturing focuses on producing a successful end product, which could be packets of chocolate biscuits or a piece of theatre. You need to understand the market-place whether you are selling from supermarket shelves or attracting a full audience.

A service is an enhancing activity. Your work does not directly produce an end product but contributes to your client's activities. This can be anything from cleaning their offices, to running a company payroll, to providing catering services. Providing a good service means understanding precisely your client's needs. In recent years services have become more specialised. A cleaning company may become particularly adept at handling industrial waste and therefore secure a more lucrative client base than a general cleaning service.

The past few years has seen greater expansion in the service sector than manufacturing. Starting up a service industry does not involve as much financial outlay as manufacturing. There may be special equipment requirements but usually services depend on the knowledge and experience of employees. The restructuring of business has resulted in some organisations ditching entire company departments and buying in services. Small- and medium-sized enterprises often cannot afford to run their own departments. Activities such as publicity or recruitment are not required all year round. Government policy on compulsory competitive tendering has brought the same business ideology to the public sector. Outsourcing can bring additional bonuses; a public relations agency will enjoy stronger links with the media than an individual department ever could.

The service sector is more people based than manufacturing and so requires stronger communication skills. Manufacturing is more technical although there are areas of crossover; a line manager on a production process will need good communication skills to motivate his staff. In both areas management roles split into three disciplines. General management controls the overall operation of the business, coordinating activities and moving the company in the right direction. Operational managers oversee particular processes; a production line, the accounts department, and so on. Finally there are service departments such as distribution, personnel and public relations, which may be intrinsic to the company or could be independent 'add-ons'. The importance and influence of each section is different for each company. Large manufacturers may be led by their production director while a service company may use different specialist staff for separate projects.

Naturally, some areas of work are more popular than others. In the 1980s marketing and public relations were especially popular. The spending boom meant the ability to influence spenders was the key to business success. Today the role has been upstaged by the buying function. Buyers locate the best suppliers – raw materials or, in the case of retail, a finished product – and secure the best deal for the company. Extensive travel gives this role some glamour, but the role has gained importance because saving money through cutting business costs is easier and more lucrative than trying to encourage more sales.

As you rise through an organisation or industry towards top-level management, you may find you are more distanced from the actual business of the company. Your first step up may mean you are dealing with the people who make the product rather than

From advising to editing

Denise Graham was a professional tax accountant working in London. She had recently completed her professional qualifications and enjoyed the work of providing advice and auditing services to large companies. However, she was beginning to find the constant pressure of work irritating and decided to find a position where work was at a slower pace so she could study tax laws and related issues in more depth. She took her knowledge and experience to a publishing house who were looking for a new editor to deal with a series of business finance titles. In this capacity, Denise found she could spend more time getting to grips with the topic. Her skills were now focused towards producing a certain product to a fixed deadline, which was in contrast to the ongoing relentless nature of her previous work. Her new job brought a whole new range of working relationships. She now liaises with fellow editors, authors, publicity staff and designers rather than simply clients who employ her services. She was able to meet more of her work colleagues face-to-face rather than just being a voice on the other end of the phone. She has a mixture of working arrangements – alone and with other people. As a tax accountant she was always under pressure to prove she was spending time on a client's case in order to justify her fee but now she could pace herself and regularly work from home rather than being tied to a desk. Her first-hand experience of the industry meant she was able to pitch her books precisely at the readership and confidently approach professionals within the industry if she needed their input. While still using the same area of knowledge, changing industries radically changed how she was working, bringing new opportunities and benefits.

making it yourself. Your next move takes you another step away from the shop-floor and so on. In some cases, promotion can stop you from doing what you want to do. In the teaching profession increased responsibilities for school management reduce the amount of time teachers spend in the classroom. Some teachers fear they will end up as little more than administrators and therefore consciously avoid promotion.

In smaller organisations specific responsibilities are harder to define and there will be few, if any, levels of management. Work is likely to be arranged on a project basis. There may be a team of people working on the same task or one individual may have sole responsibility. The production editor for a small publisher may edit copy and design the cover and layout of one book. They may also be responsible for selecting the typesetter and printer. The workload appears to be substantial compared to a large organisation where each of these functions is carried out by individual departments but the reduced bureaucracy makes the company more flexible. If the market-place changes it is easier for one person to react than to change the working priorities of several employees.

Companies are constantly assessing the effectiveness of every job in their organisation. Benchmarking activities, where the expenses and benefits of a job are measured and compared, are increasing and, as this can be as rudimentary as comparing the current salary being paid to the employee to the income specifically raised by the employee in that job, justifying your position can be stressful. There again, if you do not feel you are contributing to the overall success of the company you are unlikely to have job satisfaction.

All key employees will have expert knowledge of their particular market, and skills focused towards that market. As a prospective employee you will not be expected to have a complete understanding of a company's requirements but you must appreciate their business priorities and the priorities of the job you are taking. Recognising whether your role is manufacturing or service based will enable you to promote the relevant skills you have in that area. If you are adaptable and innovative you will be an asset to any company. You can learn the specific operation and technical aspects of your employment on the job.

WHAT WILL YOU DO:
MANUFACTURING OR SERVICE?

MANUFACTURING

- identify market opportunity
- cost of production
- cost to customer

SERVICE

- identify service requirement
- adding value to client's activity
- specialisation

MANAGEMENT OPPORTUNITIES

- general management – controlling overall operation and priorities of the business
- operational management – control over specific activities within the company
- service departments – personnel, public relations, distribution

If you have some idea of the industry in which you want to work you will know something about the positions available and the corresponding work culture. Employees may drift into their job or industry but they will not stay there if the environment does not suit them. Some areas of employment are more prescriptive than others. If you want to work in an area such as medicine, law, the police or armed forces, your career path will already be set out for you. Medical qualifications include on the job training and, once qualified, progression through the workplace is fairly clear cut. The next section of this book will therefore provide a rough guide to the less structured areas of work. This is intended as an indication of current trends and employment possibilities rather than an exhaustive job index.

WORK IN ARTS

Arts-related work is one of the most erratic areas of employment. Freelance work, self-employment and short term one-off contracts proliferate. In some areas, only the fortunate will make a living out of the specialism they studied at college. In the theatre under 10 per cent of qualified actors are in work at any one time. Many artists are determined enough to pursue their work regardless of financial reward. While this may be enough to sustain artists fresh out of college, continued rejection and the desire for a more stable lifestyle can lead to changes of direction later in their careers. However, artistic pursuits facilitate a wide skills base and lateral thinking can identify other lucrative opportunities. An artist may manage to survive selling pottery or artwork from a small studio but using the same skills in a marketing or design context could provide a greater income.

As an artist you will probably be a self-employed sole-trader. You may have recognised skills and proficiencies, but the key to success is your individuality. Writers, actors and singers have to sell their skills to production companies – publishers, directors and TV companies – and this depends on being in the right place at the right time and having the right face as much as any other factor.

The nature of the market is such that you could spend years on the poverty line or make thousands of pounds in a matter of weeks.

Visual artists face a similarly fickle market-place but at least can practice without having to rely on a producer's decision. There are many arts and craft centres where artists can gain commissions or sell pieces directly to the public from their own workshop. Work-shops often appear as part of heritage or country centres where craftspeople at work provides an additional attraction. Artistic activity can be a service or a manufacturing process but some artists believe what they do falls outside both definitions.

Rather than waiting for a producer to recognise your talent, you could set up your own company. Cooperative theatre companies or artistic resource centres can act as a service structure providing a forum for discussion and developing talent. They may also be a focus for productions. An actor's company could stage a showcase performance, a writer's collective could publish an anthology. Public and private funding for the arts is more likely to go to such groups rather than to individuals.

Many artists take casual work in order to support themselves. *The Stage* newspaper carries as many adverts for telesales and restaurant work as it does for auditions. This is a perfectly good way to pursue your career as long as your casual work does not interfere with your ideal occupation. Telesales companies like to attract actors for their oral skills and are usually sympathetic to audition appointments.

Telesales is a simple example of how artistic skills can be used in a different and lucrative way. Artists can also find opportunities in private teaching and other fields of commerce. Actors have found opportunities in business through training and assessment videos and exercises such as role-playing and mystery shoppers. Advertising thrives on creative ideas and needs artistically skilled people to originate and realise them. Designing skills are now being applied to the business world. A well designed arrangement of machinery may have great benefits in terms of increasing factory floor space.

The arts industry requires skills from all disciplines on a day-to-day basis. With increasing competition for decreasing funds there is a great demand for skilled and dedicated management staff, fund raisers and administrators. Raising money for production costs has

A stage of development

Scene One is a theatrical resource centre. It features rehearsal space, office facilities, a main stage and a gallery. The centre is funded through charity and it employs one full-time development worker and a part-time administrator. The centre's operation chiefly depends on its users: artists from all disciplines. Visiting companies perform in the theatre and there are professional exhibitions in the gallery space. Local artists use the facility as a drop in centre. They can use the office facilities for designing and producing their own promotional materials, use the rehearsal rooms to try out new material or simply to meet other like-minded people. Many of them have part-time jobs but since the centre has charitable status and charges full rates to professional users they do not have to pay to use the facilities. Recently, Scene One ran a series of arts business courses which introduced artists to the basics of becoming self-employed. These workshops provided a useful structure to focus the participant's ideas and enable them to learn from each other's experiences. The centre and the courses are also the ideal meeting place for collaborations and networking. One participant explained how he managed artistic block. Another shared her idea for a series of paintings with text and found a writer in the same session who she could work with. Although the artists do not make much money from their activities, the centre provides a strong base from which they can grow. It enhances their sense of identity and although it may be years before they are established as artists the centre means part-time subsistence work is bearable. As artists pass through it to achieve later success, the centre benefits from their experience and the publicity they bring.

always been an integral role and the National Lottery has led many organisations to attract staff with specific knowledge of how to access these funds. Management, public relations and administration roles in this area generally attract lower salaries than in other fields but employees are highly motivated by working in the artistic field.

The film and TV industries are extremely competitive and gaining work experience in this area can be very difficult. It is common to start by working for nothing and hoping this will lead to full employment. If you do get work experience you must be careful not to work unpaid for too long. After sufficient training and if you have enough contacts you may be able to work on a freelance basis in technical or creative roles as a runner, camera operator or editor. Alternatively you may be able to team up with other people and offer production companies more complete services. It is a fast moving and unforgiving industry where you will need to be aware of current trends, new projects and, most importantly, who to impress.

The BBC provides work experience in programme research and getting to know the working culture here is as important to gaining a full-time position as your talent. Many positions are advertised internally or filled by word of mouth. The corporation runs some official graduate development schemes but external adverts always attract thousands of replies. The proliferation of independent TV companies has generated further opportunities, although these can be less secure or financially rewarded than those at the BBC. There are no hard and fast rules about the industry so it is imperative to develop a good network of contacts who know what you can do and when you are available.

Uncertainty is endemic to the arts and, for some, the corresponding challenges and possibilities are a great attraction. The artistic community is better equipped to cope with an insecure job market than any other. Not only is some unemployment expected but artists can use their creative skills to cope with the situation and find new opportunities.

The industry is one of the fastest expanding areas in the economy. It has a low-cost base and the number of sole-traders setting up their own businesses is increasing. The leisure industry will continue to encourage this expansion whether through the growth of TV channels or heritage and craft centres. The technology industry is also offering a global market-place for writers, directors and performers through interactive multi-media and the Internet.

Self-employment courses have always been useful in teaching artists how to market and manage their work. Applying marketing and economic theories to artistic activities can be difficult but a degree of business discipline is essential if you are to use your creative talents in a lucrative and satisfying way. Whereas the vast majority of artists may not enjoy success, there will always be a market for creativity and originality.

WORKING WITH MONEY

Financial work is carried out in all industries and organisations, through full-time positions, consultancy work and self-employment. Creating, maintaining and measuring the flow of currency nationally and internationally can be both exciting and lucrative. In 1995, 10 per cent of all graduates went into financial work of some description.

Banking splits into retail and corporate sectors. Retail or high street banks offer similar challenges to those in other retail contexts. Customer-facing skills are required as much as financial aptitude. Banks are still able to offer structured careers and many run graduate recruitment and training programmes, which fast-track graduates to higher levels of management. A bank manager is still important for successfully running the branch but decisions on loans, mortgages and overdrafts are more commonly made by head office. The manager explains and sells financial products to the public as well as handling their day-to-day financial affairs.

Competition has led to a narrowing of the gap between high street banks and building societies and an increase in the type of products each provide. Mergers and flotations have affected many jobs and, as a result, financial organisations are always looking for new initiatives to secure an extra share of the market or to increase efficiency. Information technology has automated many transactions and increased the speed of business. The Royal Bank of Scotland was the first bank to supply insurance products over the telephone; a move which won them many customers before their competitors followed suit. Midland Bank's First Direct service led the way in telephone banking, and even that will be superseded by banking on the Internet.

This means you may never meet your customer face to face. The virtual market-place changes the types of communication skills required in the business. Providing an effective service over the telephone is different to providing one over a desk. Designing and copywriting promotional materials is extremely important if packages are to appeal to customers and be understood.

As you work through retail banking you may specialise in certain product areas. Pensions and savings specialists may be branch-based or operate through home visits. Beyond the customer interface there are the negotiators who assemble financial products and secure related deals. Insurance companies need brokers to liaise between underwriters and clients, actuaries to assess the risk of requests and set premium rates and loss adjusters to deal with claims.

Some companies have their own in-house financial department where accountants deal with the day-to-day monetary issues of the company. Alternatively, an autonomous firm of consultants may handle the financial arrangements for a range of firms, either on a daily basis or in the form of one-off audits. Self-employed accountants may run their own client list of sole-traders and small businesses. The increase in self-employment and phasing in of self-assessment means there will be no shortage of clients for this work. Many government departments employ their own accountants to control and justify their expenditure. With the right qualifications you can work in any of these situations.

The market for business-oriented financial services has increased and more specialised products are developed and implemented each year. Dedicated companies provide specific services or address single industries. Insurance companies have developed packages that provide cover for business related risks, including loss of earnings. There are many new products aimed at sole-trader companies and those working from home. Invoice discounting and factoring are aimed at improving cash-flow within companies. This service can include debt recovery and demand for both has grown due to the poor payment record of many companies. Tax accountancy can be extremely complex and is often a discrete discipline aside from other services.

Providing the right product or service to a company requires a close relationship between the financial company and the client. There may be large sums of money involved or large numbers of staff whose livelihoods will be jeopardised if the relationship fails or the product does not do what it is meant to do. There is more chance here for face-to-face contact and to get involved with the internal processes of a company, rather than matching the product to the client on the strength of an application form.

In corporate and merchant banking the amounts of money are higher; so, too, are the stress of the work and remuneration. The pressure and thrill of working in this sector is attractive and the industry is very competitive. The pressure associated with the work of stockbrokers and futures traders is legendary. Futures traders are based at the London International Financial Futures and Options Exchange where they buy and sell currency, bonds and stocks. Stockbrokers, while under less pressure, buy and sell securities in the best interests of their clients. This is where the 'Yuppies' of the 1980s made their money. The opportunities are still there today but maximum handouts go to city dealers who are able to save or make companies substantial amounts of money through managing their financial structure.

Charity work is also a financial service. Employee motivation is entirely different to that in the commercial sector, but they share the same goal of attracting public money. Successful fundraising can be seen as selling an ideal or an issue with which individuals and companies will be associated. This requires key skills in communication and promotion.

The cause provides the primary motivation for employees so charities can attract skilled employees without paying out commercial salaries. It is common for employees to remain with one campaign rather than move between organisations. Many people start their career by giving their services free to local charity offices.

Cause for a career

Jonathan Davies has worked for an international charity organisation for five years. He was first involved in a special fundraising event held by a Students' Union club while he was studying economics. Throughout his final year he worked a couple of afternoons a week at the charity's local office. He took a Masters degree, specialising in Third World Economics. During this time he helped to organise two major fundraising events, including the student initiative that had first attracted him to the charity. 'It was the first time I'd been put in a position of responsibility,' explains Davies, 'but everyone at the office were supportive and in the end we raised more money than the previous year.' Being in the office meant Davies had access to information about the organisation so would immediately know if any employment opportunities arose. When a temporary full-time campaign job came up he was able to demonstrate both the commitment and experience necessary to take the position. His years spent working voluntarily for the organisation helped him to understand how to manage his own teams of volunteers. 'You're constantly relying on the goodwill of other people,' he explains, 'and that can be quite stressful.' Davies cannot see himself doing the same kind of work for another charity: 'I don't see the work I'm doing as charity work. It's the cause that attracts me so I don't see the work as interchangeable with working for another charity.' After 18 months, Jonathan's temporary contract came to an end. Concurrently the charity decided to appoint a full-time campaigner in a different office. Davies had by now proven his worth to the organisation and his application was supported through personal recommendation from his superior at the local branch. Despite having to move geographically, he secured a full-time position with the organisation and continues to work for the cause.

The work can be extremely varied, from advocacy work and campaigning to carrying out actual relief work for the charity at home or abroad. Organisations such as Voluntary Services Overseas (VSO) direct professionals and graduates to places where they can share their talents with disadvantaged people. There are many 'eco-holidays' available where volunteers pay organisations in order to spend a number of weeks helping on nature or humanitarian projects in other countries. Although the work is rewarding it can also be tiring and frustrating. You will need to be able to inspire volunteers and the public even when you are fighting against the tide. This work attracts dedicated and hard-working people so competition for some positions can be tough.

HOTEL AND CATERING WORK

Hotel and catering work employs around 2.4 million people. Both areas have experienced economic growth over the past few years alongside other leisure industries. Aside from the obvious work environments of hotels and restaurants, the commercial sector offers opportunities in holiday camps, leisure centres, pubs, motorway services and contract catering. Dedicated catering services can be found in schools, in the travel industry – rail, airlines and cruises – as well as in hospitals and the armed forces. Skills needed by the industry go beyond food preparation and presentation to creating the overall environment where the food is served. There are many new and specialist markets appearing offering potential opportunities for creative and management staff.

You can get involved in the supply, preparation and presentation of food at many levels. You could be managing the provision of breakfast, lunch and dinner at a hotel. You could supply made-to-order sandwiches to office workers. You could even provide hundreds of three course meals at an outdoor event. While demand for mid-price restaurants is growing, this is far outstripped by the growth in fast food. Other parts of the catering industry enjoy high fashion status. Chefs and restaurants now achieve national and international reputations.

If you are serious about the kitchen and preparation side of the industry, vocational qualifications are required. These can be City and Guilds, diplomas or HCIMA (Hotel and Catering and Institutional Management Association) qualifications. You will continue to learn the trade in your first job, working your way up from the more junior and menial tasks. You may learn the trade from a respected chef but gaining experience from a wide range of establishments and situations is important if you are to prepare menus and provide excellent food to customers on a nightly basis.

Large kitchens are split into specific preparation sections and you are likely to work in each for 3–6 months before moving on. The work can be very demanding, requiring excellent organisational and communication skills over long and unsociable hours. The chief chef of a hotel restaurant may work for 70 hours a week and be on call 24 hours a day. They are also in charge of waiting staff and so have to handle any customer complaints.

Chain restaurants and hotels offer management roles for those who wish to manage the logistics of the operation. A hotel manager is responsible for all activities at their location, including entertainment and conference facilities. You may be responsible for a specific area of the operation, such as food and beverages or laundry services, or your role could be on a more national level, perhaps promoting a chain of hotels to tour operators. Whatever the size of the hotel, it is up to the management to set financial budgets, collect and work from statistical data in order to attract clients. You will need excellent leadership skills to motivate your employees and good customer-facing skills for dealing with any problems that may arise.

Running your own business in this industry is particularly challenging and should not be undertaken lightly. Setting up your own cafe or restaurant allows you to decide menus and surroundings but proprietors often find themselves working around the clock. Even when the cafe is not open you will need to organise deliveries and make preparations. Your menu must be such that the staff you employ will be able to cope with preparation if you are not on site. The enterprise can be financially precarious. Many cafes and restaurants only start making money on their menus over the long term, when the cost of supplies, building and operating are spread over hundreds of customers. Small cafes are extremely vulnerable to fluctuations in clientele. A seasonal drop in visitors due to the summer heat or to students leaving the area for the vacation could be enough to close the venture.

There are many necessary rules and regulations governing the preparation and storage of food that you will need to satisfy. There are further licensing laws governing the sale of alcohol and other activities that may take place, such as music and dancing. Successful venues are not made by menu alone but by the overall atmosphere and the people who visit. Creating the right ambience can be extremely satisfying. Cafe bars, in particular, have grown in popularity. They appeal to students and young people more than the traditional pub. In the same way as in traditional pubs, managers of cafe bars may be employed directly by a chain company, lease premises from a brewery or the property owner or could own the cafe independently. Internet cafes are appearing in every town allowing customers to surf the Web over their *cappuccino*. Vegetarian, vegan, organic and health-conscious food provide more niche markets for restaurateurs to key into. Specific vegetarian restaurants are much preferred to those that provide only one vegetarian option.

Outside catering provides a great experience for anyone interested in the industry. Corporate entertainment is extremely lucrative and if you can provide a three-course meal in the middle of the countryside in a couple of marquees, you'll probably find running a hotel kitchen easy. Such events require incredible coordination and rely on staff with great imagination and solid skills to make them happen. This also generates a lot of casual work for silver-service waiting staff. Students and graduates find this work useful and easy to fit in around other commitments. Employment agencies take on staff for the work on a temporary basis as and when they receive contracts.

Senior managers in chain restaurants and cafes are responsible for menus across the country. They need to be aware of any trends in the public's diet and be prepared for seasonal demands such as ordering thousands of turkeys months before Christmas. They need to find high-quality suppliers and negotiate the best price. Food technicians have a part to play in this process by assessing the

Food for thought

Jameson's Catering and Event Management take outside catering to the limit. From charity dinners to corporate cocktail parties, first nights of theatre performances to launches of military hardware, managing director Andrew Jameson and his team provide food and entertainment, usually for one night only, in the most unlikely venues. 'Restaurants have a two-week trial for their menus,' Andrew Jameson says. 'We don't. And if we don't get it perfect the first time, we've had it.' Getting it right requires at least two months of dedicated work. Once the menu has been decided everything else is built around providing that food. The company supplies everything from marquees and tables to audio-visual equipment and entertainment but whatever the circumstances, the crucial consideration is that the food must be served in optimum condition. A wide variety of vehicles, refrigeration and mobile preparation equipment give the team the choice of preparing food on- or off-site, whichever is best for that particular event. 'There's precise planning before-hand,' says Jameson, 'and on the day you just hope the lorry that arrives first is bringing the things you want.' This side of the industry attracts a different type of person, even among the waiting staff. 'They have to be charming and nice, but they've also got to be good team players,' explains Jameson. 'They may have to get up at 4am one morning and work through until 6am the next morning; otherwise the whole event could fall apart.' Jameson's staff are relatively young, and since this is effectively project-based work they are able to contribute to every aspect of the occasion – from transporting and erecting the marquee to clearing the crockery at the event's conclusion. 'It looks good on the CV for younger staff,' says Jameson. 'And by the time you're in your 30s you could be running your own operation or be a banquet manager in another area of the industry.'

quality and quantity of produce. Technicians are usually professionally qualified in an area of home economics and their job is to ensure the product is safe and good value for money. In addition they will design methods of preparation for the company's on-site staff using the equipment available in the restaurant chain's kitchens. The food must look and taste good but must also be easy and economic to prepare.

Knowledge of certain diets or technical details of food preparation can lead to demonstrating, teaching or writing work. The public are more informed about their diet now than ever before and are interested to know health issues and the more exotic food now available to them.

Whether you are working in your own cafe or hotel or as part of a national chain the industry is labour intensive. The larger companies still retain some career structures and there are opportunities for promotion here. Many people leave to set up their own cafes or restaurants, channelling their skills and experience towards their own personal dream.

LOCAL AND NATIONAL GOVERNMENT

The Civil Service employs around 600,000 people to develop and apply government policy to all areas of society. This area of work in government departments and related agencies can throw up unique opportunities. The diplomatic, cartographic and meteorology departments are particularly idiosyncratic. Central government recruits graduates with at least 2(ii) degrees on to their fast-track trainee scheme, but individual departments may recruit some positions directly. The skills demanded are common to those used in the private sector, from accountancy to psychology. Some of these can be applied across the full range of departments. As an accountant you could work for the Ministry of Agriculture, Fisheries and Food or, equally, with the Overseas Development Administration department.

Although job functions in the Civil Service may be similar to those in the private sector, the focus of the work is not. Government departments provide services to their particular areas of the economy and the work is more conceptual and advisory than hands on. It may also be more cutting edge and progressive; interpreting national data, assessing the effects of policies and developing new initiatives.

Another major difference between careers in the Civil Service and in private business is the structure. Financial audits and clampdowns on unnecessary bureaucracy have revolutionised some departments and continue to gnaw away at others but there remains a well structured promotion and remuneration system. There are also extensive training opportunities in skill areas such as administration, general management, communications and negotiation.

The service employs in three areas; administration, support staff and specialist workers. Basic administration work includes record keeping, filing and dealing with enquiries. Higher grades may have responsibility for managing the work of administrative sections and may assist on policy work. Support staff provide basic services to civil servants. These are manual or trade services; secretarial support, cleaning, messengers and so on. It is the area of specialist work that employs most graduates. These are the people who implement, assess and form government policy.

It is impossible to cover all types of work available in the Civil Service but the diversity of subjects covered means it is possible for you to use your skills in an area that interests you, be it a geographic location or specific topic. A good deal of the work is office-based although there can be field work, laboratory work and travel according to your responsibilities. As the European Union continues to evolve travel is likely to increase for all workers.

Part of the role of implementing and disseminating information about policies requires civil servants to attend public and private presentations. There may be consultations and presentations to be made to politicians. Civil servants essentially work for the government of the day and they must remain politically neutral. This can be a source of tension, however, if a minister is pursuing a particular line or if the media concentrate on a certain issue.

High-calibre graduates progress rapidly through their departments and are given work experience and development training to get them into higher positions quickly. These candidates have to work hard under pressure and rely on their own judgement to achieve good results.

Local government employs around three million people in the UK. The list of employees is as extensive as that for the Civil Service but, in addition, local authorities are responsible for delivering services to a geographical area. This runs from health to engineering services, housing and education to refuse collection. The government's policy of compulsory competitive tendering has led to some of these services becoming independently run companies. Offering service contracts to private companies has turned some former council departments into private or employee-owned businesses. Using market forces in this way, entrepreneurs have the opportunity to set up, bid for and run the same services.

The process began with manual services such as refuse collecting, cleaning and catering. It is now beginning to enter the professional disciplines. Library and education services are becoming more independent concerns. National departments are also in the firing line when it comes to implementing policy so changes in government priorities can mean radical changes in the workplace. While some departments are cutting back or relocating to cheaper sites outside London, others are adopting new employment structures, taking on commercial skills and business awareness alongside their professional roles.

Some local authority positions are advertised through the local press, and workplace organisation is similar to that of the Civil Service; a mixture of office-based tasks and field work. Most of the work is administrative, working policy through at a local level and ensuring the effective provision of services to a particular geographical area. Some government departments run local offices – the Central Information Office, for example, promotes specific geographical areas – so again there is the possibility of combining your skills with an area of interest or even the city where you live. Public-sector work rewards loyalty and even basic administration work in local government can lead to work at higher levels.

The Civil Service is still able to offer one of the most structured career paths in the workplace. Employees entering on lower grades can work their way up the ladder and it is one of the few environments where graduates have a clear view of their next level of

Surveying a career

Desmond McGregor graduated in planning and development surveying and went straight into a job with a local authority as a land surveyor. In this capacity he was called upon to carry out surveys for many different projects and clients, from new industrial developments to infrastructure improvements. Although he spent a good deal of time on-site taking measurements and samples for study, most of his work was office based, producing reports for clients and inquiries where land use was particularly contentious. If there was a local objection, his evidence could prove decisive in whether a development would go ahead or not. The local authority provided a framework in which to practice his skills, but after four years he decided he needed a new challenge. He secured a land surveying position with a national government department. 'The scale of projects I work on now is far larger than was ever possible with the local authority,' he explains. 'The local authority gave me the chance to use my skills on a practical basis, but now I really feel I'm contributing to the industry in general.' The government department is at the cutting edge of producing and using digital map data and therefore uses up to the minute technology to map out locations. The use of satellite location systems, computers and other technology means McGregor's current work is radically different from that which he carried out with the local authority, even though he's still using the same basic skills. McGregor now works alongside practitioners across Europe in developing and using Geographic Information Systems.

responsibility and the appropriate pay grade to match. There can be a lot of bureaucracy to negotiate in the job and this can be frustrating and slow down your work rate. There is a danger here, as with all long-term single employer work, that you become so used to operating within your particular environment that you cannot transfer your skills to another situation. You must be careful not to become complacent or institutionalised. The security and protection given by a government department can mean some workers would find it difficult to adapt their work to the commercial market.

COMMUNICATIONS

In the global market-place the key to attaining the competitive edge is efficient communications. If you can get your message, product, money or knowledge around the world before anyone else then your company will be a market leader. For this reason jobs in communication related areas are extremely important. As technology and customer expectations from technology push forwards, all jobs evolve and change.

Information technology has many applications in diverse industries. Moreover, as the equipment becomes cheaper and more accessible, new situations where it can bring benefits emerge. The Internet allows companies to transfer data across all international barriers. It is a shop-front for the global market, allowing companies to communicate directly with their customers on a daily basis. Once online, a sales department in America can easily push a product to buyers in Australia. Internet technology is being used for internal company communications. Intranets share information between company departments regardless of their geographic location.

Computer jobs in the UK have always been service based rather than in manufacturing. For this reason the job market depends on how companies implement the technology rather than how much they buy. The late 1980s saw a reduction in demand but this has reversed as costs have fallen. Today, computer technologists work on many different projects, applying technology in ways that will allow companies to operate more efficiently and effectively.

The nature of the work usually means computer consultancies have very little employment structure, they simply provide the most suitably qualified worker for each project. You do not need to be a scientific genius to secure employment in this area. There are post-graduate conversion courses which give the necessary skills to apply the technology and learn computer programming regardless of your first degree. Even if you have an arts background you may have the imagination and aptitude for providing information technology solutions to business problems.

The more traditional side of the communications industry is still thriving. Promoting a company or client through brand image, design, copywriting, press releases or an advertising campaign is a creative and technical task. Advertising is thought to be a very young industry but it is possible to build a long-term career as long as your ideas remain in demand.

A company may employ its own marketing department to generate interest in new products and the company in general. There may also be a press officer responsible for company appearances in the media and for handling any enquiries which may arise from company activity, maintaining its image and countering negative publicity. This role is sometimes taken by an independent marketing company. Public relations agencies represent a number of companies, sometimes from similar industries. This means they can concentrate on developing closer links with the media, coordinating interviews and photo-shoots to the advantage of both the media and the company.

All these areas need great communication skills – oral and written – organisational skills, tact, diplomacy and the ability to ensure projects are completed on time and within budgets. Employees need boundless enthusiasm for the product or company they represent and lots of creativity. Developing new angles and promotional ideas demands a degree of lateral thinking, especially if you need to come up with great ideas under pressure of deadlines. This always requires teamwork and there is plenty of negotiation between the client and creative staff, and even between company directors who may have different ideas about how the company and product should be promoted.

Loud and clear

Holly Summers went travelling for a year after she graduated from university with an engineering degree. She decided she wanted to work in a people-oriented environment rather than a purely scientific one. She secured a job with a small company of business consultants in London. The company describes themselves as a public relations and communications company and make extensive use of their own technical expertise when addressing clients. One of Holly's first projects was for an industrial manufacturing company who wanted to counter recent negative press reports. Rather than simply dreaming up a new positive image and selling this to the public, Holly conducted extensive research into the company's practice. She asked employees and customers where they thought improvements could be made. She used this information, together with skills from her degree, to construct an extensive improvement plan for the company's executive. The research also meant she could create a new image for the company which precisely met the criticisms made by customers. In order to make the executive board accept these ideas she had to make the report attractive and positive, emphasising the benefits these changes would bring rather than the problems she had identified. Alongside this project she was also involved in identifying new work opportunities for the company, constructing bids for other contracts and taking part in presentations to secure new contracts. The company sponsored her through a Chartered Institute of Marketing course, a task that proved difficult early on as she was getting used to the work and trying to study at the same time. 'I think this work allows me to use all my skills, not just the knowledge my degree gave me,' she explains. 'You're working on something different every day. You may be interviewing people, researching, writing or presenting. Because we're a small company, everyone knows which projects are being worked on at the time and we are able to discuss the issues and bounce ideas off each other.'

Employees must be up to date with the media and current trends in contemporary society. The predicted explosion of cable and digital television will bring a wealth of new markets directly into the customer's home. Interactive TV will also be a new way to sell. Advertising space on the Internet is already generating income for some companies. If you are to communicate effectively you must be aware of the signals given by certain colours, music and images and how these affect your product's appeal to a particular customer.

Communications technology is creating new opportunities for many graduates. Companies are already employing writers to design and manage home pages on the Internet. The proliferation of mobile phones and pager services has generated a new and lucrative market-place. Cable companies are connecting private houses and businesses, creating opportunities for technical staff, engineers and scientists and expanding the market for entertainment production companies. Such is the rate and nature of change that it is impossible to forecast the companies, services and opportunities that will appear in the future. From cable shopping to videophones the communications industry will thrive on the professionals who know how it works and how to improve it, and provide work for those who have the insight and imagination to exploit it.

Communications also includes transport. Despite becoming a more knowledge-based economy there is still a demand for swift and effective transportation of people and freight by road, rail and air. The new market-place is making more and more demands on international freight and next day delivery. There is a constant need for fleet management to coordinate the journey of freight around the world.

There is much competition for passengers in the air and on the roads. The deregulation of public transport, particularly bus services, has produced many new transport companies at local and national level. Rail privatisation has brought market forces to the network and although it is still relatively new the reorganisation has already changed many jobs. Transport companies need management staff to timetable services, cost them out and oversee day-to-day operation. Airlines are bigger organisations and have many operational departments and separate management disciplines, from general management tasks to scheduling flights and training cabin crew.

Whatever job or industry you work in you will have to deal with communications technology in some way. Electronic mail, fax machines and modems may not have rendered the postal service useless but have shown how technology can completely change an activity. There is much speculation over what the Internet will become and it is imperative that you stay aware of the possibilities in your industry. It is infinitely better to be one step ahead of developments rather than always trying to keep up.

CONSTRUCTION WORK

The working culture of the construction industry can be a great deterrent. The popular conception of building sites is of male-dominated, dangerous places to work. While it is difficult to contribute to the industry without spending some time on site the industry does offer many creative and technically demanding jobs for professionals. The size of the industry is immense, covering everything from the planning of a local shopping mall to investigating possible oil sites in the North Sea to building a private extension. The essential qualifications of engineering and science-related degrees are in demand in all areas and further training can lead to specialist work.

The industry is high cost and high risk and the recession hit the trade hard. Building an office block can be financially disastrous if the owner cannot lease out the building. Falling house prices mean there is less investment in new homes. The government is looking more and more to private investors to fund infrastructure projects. The more professional roles, architects, designers and surveyors, have been less affected than the manual builders, as a contractor still wants to know what a project will look like and how much it will cost whether or not he has the money to carry out the work.

Most work in the industry is project based and there may be complicated contracting and subcontracting arrangements between a number of companies on any single project. All construction workers must be flexible in their approach to work, as problems may arise in communication and coordination. The work can be stressful when a project needs to be completed to a deadline and within a strict budget, and can mean irregular and unsociable hours. Motorway maintenance is sometimes scheduled overnight in order to cause minimum disruption to traffic. This aspect of the work prevents many women from following unbroken careers in the industry. There is no reason why anyone should work under such difficult conditions. Initiatives are under way to encourage more women into the industry (they currently make up less than 10 per cent of the million-strong workforce), to attract ethnic minorities and to promote better working practices generally.

Qualifying as an architect takes around six years of study, including a year spent in practice. Gaining the practical year out has become increasingly difficult as larger numbers of students compete for the same number of opportunities. Architects are involved with construction projects from their very conception. Whether extending a private house or building a new office block they will be the first to consider the possibilities. This means liaising with the client and considering the feasibility and ecological impact of the construction. Once construction is under way, the architect visits the site to ensure the work is going according to plan and to sort out any problems. The task requires great interpersonal skills as well as clear conceptual thinking.

Alongside the architect there are many specialist workers responsible for managing the necessary materials and manpower. Quantity surveyors make accurate estimates for material resources. Other surveyors inform planners and architects of geographical features they need to consider. There are specialist surveyors of land, marine, mineral and hydrographic features, all of whom can be called upon for advice and help.

Design is another part of the construction industry where both the large scale and smallest detail are important. Designers help to shape specific products for the home and street, furniture and lighting as well as creating general environments. They provide input on the appearance of public places, balancing necessary safety and functional requirements with production costs and aesthetic qualities. Computer-aided design programs help designers develop their

Building a career

Jan Preston's career officer did not approve when she professed an interest in taking a three-year course in building studies, but Jan had always been fascinated by buildings and how they were put together. As her course progressed she found her interest to be stronger than the disincentive of working in a potentially hostile, all-male culture. In fact, having always associated her work with this culture, her treatment on-site was never a problem. She is now an architectural technician for a design and build consultancy. The firm deals with relatively small-scale construction work; private extensions, village halls, and so on. Jan enjoys the creative planning stages of each project, but seeing the original plans become reality provides immense satisfaction. 'When you see all the resources you are bringing together in order to make this possible you get a great sense of achievement,' she explains. Her work means that once a project is under way she has to leave her desk and supervise on-site activities. She will discuss practical problems with her architectural colleagues, surveyors and technicians from other organisations, but unless she is able to communicate her decisions to the workers themselves there are likely to be further complications. 'Day-to-day hands-on management is performed by the foreman,' notes Jan, 'and they go at the work from a purely technical point of view.' While this may be at the expense of aesthetic details and sometimes the opinions of the other workers on the project, Jan enjoys the variety of work and views that one project can produce. Working environments and hours vary according to the project undertaken. The size and type of building brings different challenges; constructing a completely new building is radically different to adding another room to the back of a house. However, since most contracts carried out by the firm are for private customers Jan's working hours are fairly flexible and rarely unsociable.

ideas in three dimensions without having to build scale models. The programs can also work out how much material is required for a particular product.

You will find work in a wide range of employment structures. You may be able to operate as a self-employed freelance consultant. You may be part of an architectural practice and become a partner later in your career. Civil engineering work is centred on the design and construction of public facilities. This work, concerning itself with road and town planning, may be carried out at central government or local government level.

Interior design offers more opportunities for designers and architects as well as providing a market for people with appropriate skills in decorating. Skilled workers may be self-employed or team up with other people to provide a full service. Private clients may employ decorators and craftspeople with skills from thatching to special painting skills; stippling, rag rolling, and so on. These services can command respectable fees if not constant work. Some artists specialise in large paintings for commercial and private spaces. For example, a painter may be commissioned to design and paint a mural in a restaurant.

The industry offers the chance of foreign travel and many construction companies are finding new work and partnerships with companies in Eastern Europe, Asia and Russia. Russia offers many opportunities as native companies are only just learning how to operate in a free market and how to tender for construction contracts. Firms from the west can share their skills and are finding work over there to be more lucrative than at home.

Whether involved in the design, tendering process, site preparation or actual construction work, the sheer scale of activity in terms of manpower, logistics and final product is staggering. One only has to look at some recent achievements, the Channel Tunnel or the extension of the Jubilee underground line, to understand that completing a construction project must surely be one of the most satisfying feelings. No other industry affects our environment in such a way or so radically alters the skyline.

THE LEISURE INDUSTRY

The leisure industry is the fastest growing industry in the UK. Sports and recreation activities alone employ around 400,000 people, but there are always new products and services appearing to help people get away from it all, relax or simply fill in a few hours of spare time. We now have more leisure time and spending power for that time than ever before. Both manufacturing and service businesses are common to the industry, providing tour guides, package holidays and specialist equipment for the most obscure hobby.

In 1970 there were about 20 sports centres nationally. Today there are 1500. Most are privately owned but some are still run by local authorities. These establishments need managers and trainers, swimming pool lifeguards and other activity-specific staff. There are vocational leisure management courses but this is an area of work you could enter through your personal interest rather than through academic qualifications. While at college many students are involved in sporting pastimes and, whereas only a few go on to practise the sport professionally, sporting talent can be productively shared with others.

Private centres and health clubs employ fitness trainers, coaches and instructors. The same jobs can be found at hotels, holiday camps and outward-bound centres. Vocational qualifications and recognition from a sport's governing body may be necessary for you to work. Some positions can be part-time or self-employed. Personal trainers may be attached to a sports centre or could equally work on a freelance basis. Leisure and sport centres also require general managers to run facilities and oversee individual departments. This area demands the usual skills in personnel management and customer-facing situations. Good administration and negotiating skills are also needed, particularly if facilities are shared by different groups.

If you are employed at a local authority owned centre there will be more of a structured career path open to you, or at least a reliable pay scale, but given the limited size of many of these centres, increased responsibilities and remuneration may only be possible if you move to another location. Alternatively, you could rise through the management structure to a position such as recreational officer where you will be responsible for coordinating the general provision of facilities throughout your geographical area. A career in the private sector is open to the usual market pressures and your development and progress will depend largely on your own reputation in your profession.

Tourism provides jobs in sending travellers abroad and offering services to those who visit this country. Travel agents are the retail side of the industry but selling this product is far more customer-oriented than any other high street outlet. Holidays are a major investment for the customer, who will have been saving up and looking forward to getting away for many months. If the trip is not what was expected refunds or exchanges are not going to help. There is a great difference between supplying tailor-made, independent travel for students and young people and offering family packages. Some travel agents send their own staff out to assess the resorts and determine the ideal customer for certain trips.

The industry has a fashion side to it, with resorts becoming popular one year and falling out of popularity the next. Out of the way and exotic resorts gradually become part of the mainstream as new developments are built, more flights scheduled and prices fall. A few years ago Turkey was considered a novel destination. Today, parts of Turkey are completely commercialised and it is a popular destination for families from all over Europe. Senior travel agency managers must be fully aware of these trends in order to negotiate well with suppliers.

Business travel is another market altogether, both in terms of the products offered and the retail transaction. Trips are usually arranged over the phone rather than face to face so operators must be sure to get the right details every time. Large retail companies offer many opportunities in management, publicity, training and customer services.

As a tour manager or courier you travel with holiday makers to ensure their trip goes smoothly and that they have an enjoyable time. Alternatively, holiday representatives may stay at one location to look after tourists as they arrive and to arrange activities and excursions. This area of work usually requires fluency in a foreign language, as you will be liaising between English-speaking

A travelling career

American studies graduate, Dave Pearce, took his first job in a temporary telesales position with a major supplier of business holidays. He spent his working day on the phone taking customer orders and matching their demands with arrangements available through the Galileo Focal Point. This database holds the details of flights, hotels and many other holiday products and allows operators to research and book excursions through one terminal. At first Pearce believed the job would last only two or three years after which he would have enough money to go travelling himself, but as time went on he found the industry more and more attractive. 'I was offered other training opportunities by the company,' he explains, 'and that inspired my interest.' The office is arranged in teams of salespeople, each allocated a certain number of business accounts. Pearce was promoted to team leader and was then given the opportunity to go on the company's management training course. 'It hadn't occurred to me before but there were all sorts of areas to the company you just don't see from outside,' he says. 'You could join the personnel department, planning, buyers, the training department or even the technology department.' It was the last department to which Pearce was particularly attracted. A few months later he helped to introduce new technology to the national office that automated the sending of tickets to customers, saving office space and reducing the time from sales to dispatch. 'I never thought I'd stay in this industry,' confesses Pearce, 'but in a way the work I do now actually has very little to do with selling holidays itself. It's about managing the equipment the company uses and ensuring it operates to maximum efficiency.'

tourists and local providers. This work is available during the summer months and at ski resorts during winter. Dealing with irate customers can be difficult and the remoteness of your location can add to the stress. You may find you do not even have time to explore the country you are working in. Many graduates find temporary summer work in holiday camps in America and Europe and return year after year, using the work as a springboard for further travel.

UK heritage and tourist centres require administrators, receptionists and guides to help foreign tourists. Some locations include exhibitions and virtual reality experiences among their attractions. There are new opportunities for historians and designers in bringing the past to life in a way that interests and stimulates visitors. Even museums are losing their stuffy academic image, becoming more interactive and user friendly.

Theme parks continue to enjoy popularity. There are many different roles at these centres, from general management to catering services, designing special events and providing customer services. Some parks even employ performers to entertain customers in and around the park's attractions.

Leisure activities include managing facilities such as national parks, outward-bound centres, multi-screen cinemas and nightclubs as well as providing for all manner of hobbies from fly-fishing to bungee jumping. Providing and managing these kinds of facilities can be done on a freelance self-employed basis or you could work in one branch of a large organisation. An active interest in the area is of equal importance to a professional qualification. Despite its expansion and overall security, the industry is susceptible to sudden changes in taste and you must remain in touch with trends to generate work. It is one industry where your work is someone else's pleasure.

THE RETAIL INDUSTRY

Retail work covers all areas where goods or services are sold to the public. Customer relations are only one aspect of the industry.

Behind the scenes there are a whole host of roles in buying, selling and merchandising. Market research also plays a key role in servicing the industry, giving advance information on likely customers and measuring the success of a product. Retail is a labour-intensive industry where fashion and trends must be predicted months in advance and niche markets identified and promoted. Aside from the conventional supermarket and department store, home shopping is on the increase through catalogues and, more recently, TV and the Internet. The industry employs around two million people, 45 per cent of whom are part-time. It is easy to get work experience in the sector; you may have already have had experience on the shop floor in a Saturday job or worked in telesales.

Retail outlets vary in size and type. Small, local, owner-managed shops may offer opportunities for speciality selling. These include antique shops, chemists and bookshops. Alternatively you may be able to set up your own enterprise or go into business as a co-op with others. At the other end of the industry are the limited companies, national and multinational outlets. The size of these shops, often located out-of-town, is impressive and managers can find themselves in charge of hundreds of staff and the daily restocking of thousands of lines.

Management roles on shop-floor level are broadly similar whatever the chain-store. Store managers can expect to be on their feet for most of the day, dealing with staff and customers, and ensuring that deliveries arrive on time and that shelf stackers are there to deal with them. There are some differences, however, according to the types of products you are selling.

The fastest moving area of retail is food. Supermarkets hold an incredible number of lines and generate a rapid turnover of stock. There are many different sections to each store, as well as dedicated support staff including everyone from the personnel department to the staff canteen. Managers may begin in charge of specific business departments, finance, deliveries or even separate areas of produce. These departments may require extra qualifications, in food and hygiene for example, which can be gained on the job. Branches of large chain stores are run as discrete businesses with the general managers ultimately responsible for the success of the stores. The manager needs to be aware of all aspects of the business. The size and diversity of a large store, with annual and weekly changes in stock and new lines, provide very challenging long-term work.

Barcode technology has revolutionised the shopping experience. Staff can access up-to-date information on stock levels and reordering is fully automated. In the future, check-outs may be replaced by customers entering the codes themselves. Information from all branches is collated and fed to the corporate office staff who make decisions on everything about the branches, from product lines to store layout. They can measure week-by-week how much of a product has sold nationwide and regionally. As well as measuring their current success this information is particularly important to planners, buyers and merchandisers to help them predict future trends.

Working many months in advance, buyers will decide what customer demand will be in the future and locate the best quality products. They may work on an individual range, such as a new line in boyswear for summer, or they may be responsible for the entire stock of a small department, such as kitchenware. Again, the product they work on determines the speed and nature of that work. Buyers may travel all over the world to find new suppliers or simply to view what is going into shops internationally. They attend fashion shows and factories, making carefully balanced decisions on goods according to the quality and price and the reliability of the supplier. The merchandiser and planner works with the buyer in planning the entry of the product into stores nationwide. This will include presentation, price and stock levels. When the goods go into the store the team will monitor their progress, reordering or repricing goods as necessary.

Price-wars, reward cards and new product lines are all designed to attract customers to the store and guarantee they keep coming back. The rise of 'own-brand' labels is one area where managers can directly contribute to the profitability and popularity of a store. Store layout is also very important in creating the right atmosphere for shoppers.

Market research can offer a long term career as well as throwing up useful opportunities for lucrative part-time or temporary interview work. The industry is small and specialist, which means there

Shopping for a career

Jason Freeman is a buyer for a high street retail chain-store. He graduated with a good degree in business studies and was taken onto the company's management trainee course. 'The first thing they do is put you into the shops,' he says. 'After all, if you don't have a clear idea of what happens on the shop-floor, you can't really begin to understand how the business works.' Jason found, however that he did not enjoy the work in this area of the business. He enjoyed helping people but felt frustrated by the lack of control he had over the products that appeared on the shelves. During a feedback interview with his development manager, it was suggested he should try for one of the positions in head office, either as a buyer or a merchandiser. He undertook a six-month secondment to head office and found he instantly clicked with the role of buyer. 'It's the antithesis of the 9-to-5 job,' says Freeman. 'It can be extremely exhausting, but the fact that you're involved with so many aspects of bringing a product to the stores nationwide is very exciting.' Freeman travels for the company for about ten weeks in every year. The rest of the time he is negotiating supply arrangements or liaising with planners and merchandisers in order to introduce the product to the stores in the most effective way. Freeman therefore needs to have a wide range of skills, from individual initiative and research skills to teamwork abilities. 'I've gained a huge range of skills with the company in all kinds of fields, both through formal courses and on-the-job training,' he says. 'The scope of the buying role is extremely broad. It's not just about the product, the focus is on producing a profitable range and that requires extensive business knowledge.'

are lucrative opportunities for graduates with the right qualifications and aptitude. Research requires excellent communication skills, principally to establish what each client expects from the research and then to get an unbiased response from the public. Designing questionnaires, interviewing by telephone or face to face, or leading a discussion group on a particular topic are all techniques used to collect information and opinions. Knowledge of a computer language is often important so that facts and figures can be collected, analysed and presented effectively.

Large retail companies take on graduates every year but the trainee management courses are always swamped by applications. If you are lucky enough to be accepted on the course it will offer you great experience and useful skills applicable to many areas of work. Graduates are a great source of new ideas for the industry and flatter personnel structures and team work enable them to put forward new initiatives. Recruits are brought into the counter culture swiftly, and frequently study for vocational marketing qualifications through classroom and home study. The demand for skilled graduates in this sector over recent years has led to a good deal of competition between stores to find, attract and retain the best candidates.

WORK IN EDUCATION

Teaching is very popular among graduates, with some students immediately going into the classroom and some postponing for a year or so. Others come to the profession having already had a career in another area of work. Most teachers take a year's Post Graduate Certificate of Education (PGCE), which provides full training in the classroom and grooms students for the rigours of the state education system. However, graduates can find employment in the private sector and even at higher and further education levels without any additional training.

Teachers in secondary and further education usually teach the subject they studied at college although alongside this they need to offer a second subject. Most employers require a teacher to cover two subjects and you should be careful in your selection of subjects to ensure they are complimentary and useful to schools. Primary and infants classes are structured differently and teachers here are expected to teach a range of subjects to their tutorial group. It is important to identify the age group you want to teach since the rewards of the job vary with the children's age.

Full-time teaching is rewarding but it is no soft option. If you consider only the period of time spent in pupil-to-tutor contact then the perception is one of long holidays and short working days. However, there are many hours spent on lesson planning, marking books and working on extra-curricula activities. Teaching may extend into evening classes during term time. Preparations for exams or even events such as Christmas concerts can take over entire weeks. The subject you teach will dictate your workload and the skills and knowledge you need. The school's location will also influence your job. The skills and energy levels required to interest kids from an inner city area are different to those needed to motivate a rural community classroom.

There is more to the job than standing up and sharing your enthusiasm for a subject. You must be able to maintain discipline within the classroom and be sensitive to the needs of individual pupils. Schools and colleges are an important focus for the local community and their facilities are used by many different groups.

Career structures within state education are fairly well defined. Salary increases each year with experience, and taking on extra responsibilities within schools also earns additional pay. The ability to manage staff and facilities is important and can move you up the career ladder, but many teachers find such career progression often means moving further away from the classroom and towards management and administrative duties.

A headteacher may still teach in the classroom but will need skills in personnel management and even finance to oversee the smooth running of the school. The education system is very high profile and is constantly debated and reorganised by the political parties. The national curriculum places demands on every teacher to fulfil certain requirements. It can be very stressful to work in such an atmosphere where public expectations are high.

The political debate even extends to the way in which PGCEs are taught. The trend has been to get trainees into the classroom as soon as possible so they have to cope with the practical situation and learn from experience. This can be very daunting and can make or break a student early on. Teaching is a vocation, requiring a certain aptitude rather than the ability to learn a certain skill. Once qualified, employment is not guaranteed and the ease of getting a first job will depend on your subject and the geographical area in which you want to work. The more flexible you are, the easier you will find it to gain employment.

PGCEs are offered by many institutions and are available at the Open University through distance learning. Science and mathematics teachers are currently in short supply and attract extra financial awards from the government. There are also courses aimed specifically at training teachers to teach older students or within evening classes. This form of teaching is more attractive to some people since in theory you can concentrate on teaching the subject without having to deal with classroom discipline.

Private schools take on subject specialists who may have no official teaching qualifications. The skill requirements are still the same although pay and conditions vary. You may find yourself resident on the premises if it is a boarding school. Private tutelage can be conducted from your own home or you may prefer to be peripatetic and travel from client to client in order to teach lessons. Clients could be local schools and institutions or individual private students. Teaching on a one to one basis or to a small group is popular for music and language teachers. There are many more opportunities for private tuition around exam time when students need to brush up on their skills or cram in more knowledge.

Teaching English as a foreign language opens up many opportunities internationally and TEFL courses provide a useful qualification if you wish to work in this area. With these recognised qualifications you can travel around the world and support yourself on a long-term basis through teaching. There are many ex-pat communities in the major cities of Europe and beyond, working in areas of commerce and industry. English is an international business language and many foreign companies and organisations are keen that their employees learn it as quickly as possible. There are opportunities from private tuition of children to coaching

Teaching all over the world

Helen Parker graduated from an Italian course four years ago and has been working round the world teaching English as a foreign language. She developed many contacts with Italy at college, spending a year there as part of her studies, and this was where she first went after graduation. She had previously worked as a nanny in Rome and knew of a couple of language schools that would be interested in her skills. At the same time she knew the local English community so felt confident she would be able to find somewhere to live and work. 'I felt I would make a good teacher, but preferred to teach adults and to be somewhere outside the UK,' she explains. After eight months of teaching at one of the language schools she returned to England and took a TEFL course in London. The course was intensive and gave her extra confidence as well as further contacts for her work. The school has since offered her work to teach her skills to other TEFL students in England because she proved to be such a successful student. Her new qualification opened up a wide range of possibilities. She has worked in Japan and Spain, travelling around Europe and further afield when holidays and finances permit. 'I'm still addicted to travelling,' she says. 'I get itchy feet every 6 months and teaching English has enabled me to stay in many places I would not have otherwise seen.' Helen's work has not only been limited to schools. In Madrid she found herself coaching the English accents of television presenters, and while in Rome she was able to find lucrative translation work. 'This was particularly rewarding as I could do the work whenever I wanted to rather than being called upon to work at certain times of the day.' In the future she hopes this translation work will lead to more long-term employment in international business communications.

businessmen. If you are already fluent in another language you may not need a TEFL qualification although you will still need the ability to structure courses and help your students constructively.

Further and higher education is a more specialist area of work. Tutors and lecturers are expected to carry out ongoing research into their subjects and to regularly publish their findings. Recently it appears that funding has depended more on this side of departmental activity than on the service given to students. Entrance to this side of education tends to be through postgraduate study, with graduates taking on tutorial groups or teaching certain areas of a course while completing diplomas. You will learn more about teaching in higher and further education contexts this way than you will through conventional teaching qualifications. As your career progresses you will be expected to achieve higher qualifications yourself while making important contributions to your field of interest.

As with all teaching posts a level of bureaucracy exists alongside the work. Lecturers need to process and select new students each year, assess their progress and tend to their needs and pastoral concerns. Working within an institution can be a very exciting environment offering financial security while you research your pet subject.

PART THREE

YOU

WHO YOU ARE

The fractured nature of the job market means that creating a career is your own responsibility. There are few employers in a position to train and develop graduates and fewer still who can guarantee long-term employment. Not only must graduates make the first move in securing employment, but they need to put together an entire career campaign that will serve for many years to come. This places additional responsibilities on graduates compared to previous generations but it can also be seen as an extremely positive feature. In theory you can enter whatever profession you desire; all you need to do is prove your interest, hone your talents and dedicate yourself to that industry or position.

Unfortunately, complete freedom of choice can present its own difficulties. How can you make any decision if you have a limited idea of what specific jobs entail and what possibilities are open to you? It can be difficult to find the motivation to engage in the world of work, especially after so many years of education. On the other hand you may have useful talents you are keen to use but do not know where or how to apply those talents.

Creating your career is not simply a matter of deciding what job you want. You must consider other aspects of your life as well. Your desires and expectations from life will help to determine what you need from employment and help you recognise the opportunities available. At the moment you may have no long term goals or expectations. This is not a bad thing; you simply need to be aware that the decisions you take now are based on short term expectations. As you grow older your priorities will change and you will need to adapt your career path to accommodate these changes.

The advantage of the new project-based and short-term work career structure is that it gives you maximum flexibility. You have control of where you go, what you do and why. You could take a relatively boring project because the remuneration means you can subsequently work on a project which is not so lucrative but far more enjoyable. The new model means there is no excuse for stagnating or becoming trapped in an area of work you do not like.

The most long-term consideration that influences your career is your lifetime dream. What is your overriding ambition? You may dream of representing your country in the Olympics, or of being a film star or celebrity. You may have the talent, connections and motivation to attain that position but even if your dream is unobtainable it can still provide clues to where you could work. Think carefully about your dream and identify what it is about the idea that makes it appealing. Is it the financial reward or the activity itself? Is it the lifestyle that comes with the work? From this you can identify areas of work that either provide similar qualities or enable you to attain those things. If you want to be a pop star you may find an unrelated job that supports you while you practice your music. Alternatively you could use those skills to teach music and find satisfaction through working with music every day. A dream job can be a long- or short-term goal, but the aspects of the work that you find attractive will remain attractive for much longer.

You can use your dream no matter how unobtainable it is. Wishes, on the other hand, are goals that are obtainable. Where do you see yourself in 10 or 20 years time? It could be impossible to think of the job you will have, but you may be able to picture where you will live, how you will be living, and who you will be living with. Will you have a family, a mortgage, two cars and holiday in the south of France? Are you more concerned to be working in a particular job or industry by the time you reach that stage?

It may seem a long way away but if you know how you feel about these aspects of your life you will be able to create a career that enables you to achieve what you desire. If you want to support a family you will need an amount of security, work-wise and financially. This does not mean finding the elusive job for life, but ensuring your skills are up-to-date and constantly in demand from employers. This may be more important to you than the area of work in which you are involved. If your wish is to be a senior executive by the time you are forty then you can start working towards that now, listing the skills and experience you will need to get there and finding roles and employers who will set you off in the right direction.

Most wishes have a time-scale attached to them; travel the world this year, move house in two years' time and have a family in ten. You can plan your career around these events. You may work anywhere for a year to earn enough money to travel next year. If you are starting a family, you will need to plan for all the related expenses or ensure you are geographically secure while your children go through important stages in their education. You can create a rough guide of what you need to achieve and when you need to achieve it by and use this to indicate the type of work and career structure you need.

Conflicts can appear between wishes and you may need to prioritise. Some work will simply not pay enough money to support the lifestyle you desire. You will have to decide whether the work is satisfying enough, or whether you need to find a more lucrative activity. You may decide to work to support a family over the first ten years of your career and then move into your choice area of work when family demands have subsided. Be aware, however, that some industries thrive on the talents of new graduates and failure to get involved or to pick up certain knowledge at this stage may jeopardise your ambitions of joining the profession later in life.

You will need to achieve a balance between what you do for a living and the rest of your life. If you are fortunate you may find a job that satisfies you as much as your leisure pursuits. Work that addresses a hobby or personal interest can do this. For most people, however, there is a payoff between what they do for a living and the things they enjoy doing as a result of that work. You may feel put upon because you have to work late but the extra money means you can take your family to America this year instead of the Isle of Wight. Alternatively, you may find your work leaves no time for socialising at all but it doesn't matter because you love what you do.

Both scenarios are acceptable ways to live and work. Problems only occur if you are not happy with the rewards gained from the job. As you grow older and your career progresses your priorities will alter and the balance will change. You may achieve some wishes and disregard others. A top sales executive may spend ten years working hard before deciding it is time to settle down and start a family. The move will completely change working arrangements and while others believe this is 'dropping out' of the competitive world of work, the executive will view it as a positive move and be entirely satisfied with the new arrangements.

If you have no strong dreams or wishes there are other ways of determining your first and subsequent career moves. Every job you take will use the skills you have and develop new skills. By auditing your skills you can identify areas in which you are particularly suited and which will challenge and develop your skills. Assessing your skills and aptitudes indicates where to look for work in the short term and may suggest long-term aims. Excellent communication skills could secure a temporary telesales job. The same skills could result in a long-term career in marketing.

Making career choices on the basis of the skills you have and those you want practically guarantees job satisfaction and makes any industry your potential employer. Working in order to gain and improve skills can be more satisfying than being under-employed even in your preferred industry. If you have a strong idea of what you want to do, assessing your skills base is crucial. Realising strengths and weaknesses now will mean you can work on the skills you need in order to achieve your dream job.

You must discuss your skills with other people. We all tend to underrate our abilities and sometimes miss out whole areas that other people think are important. Family, friends or tutors are useful for this. Finding out what other people think of you need not be embarrassing or formal. A casual chat on a shared interest may lead to someone making a comment about your ideas which has a crucial bearing on what kind of person you are. Try and get as many viewpoints as possible. The more talents you can identify and the clearer your view of your skills the more employable you become. Employers want someone with a rounded personality and a variety of interests; someone who is enjoyable to work with. Your views on football or the music industry may secure your employment rather than intricate industry knowledge.

Your academic subject has given you specialist knowledge but need not dictate your area of work. Having studied one subject for a number of years you may decide it's time for a break. More important to take away from your college career is to understand the way in which you have learned. Are you a great note taker, do you remember everything someone tells you, or do you learn by experience, trial and error? If you can find a working environment that mirrors this learning pattern you will be happier and more productive.

Consider all your extra-curricula interests; the clubs, social events and occasions you have taken part in. Think about how you fit into these situations. Are you constantly at the centre of operations, keen to arrange everyone else or on the periphery, happy to join in but uncomfortable in taking the initiative? Your involvement in running these events may directly relate to an employment situation or the activity will illustrate skills and aptitudes employers want. Charity or voluntary work is particularly good since it proves social and political awareness, a high level of motivation and good interpersonal skills.

Presenting your skills effectively to an employer is incredibly important. If possible you should adapt your CV for each job, increasing the emphasis on elements pertaining to that particular position. You may decide to present the information in a different order for different employers. Teamwork experience may be important for one employer, but another may require vocational skills. Make sure you understand what the employer's advert or recruitment literature is asking for; both your CV and accompanying letter should address these aspects first.

Personalising your CV for each application can be difficult without wordprocessing facilities. Even if you do not have access to these facilities you should spend a significant amount of time on your CV. A clear and rational layout and concise text is as important as the content. Your CV should emphasise experience and skills rather than academic prowess and employment positions.

Working life can be very boring if you are not challenged. If you can do the work standing on your head it is unlikely to hold your attention and ultimately your work will not be of the highest quality. Preparing your CV may highlight areas of work where you could improve or develop your skills. You can therefore select your first job on the basis of the skills and challenges it offers you. What the job is and what industry you are working in matters less than the function you carry out.

Even after looking at your skills you may still have no idea what kind of work to apply for. This means you have no expectations, preferences or limitations for your work. Not knowing what you want to get out of life can be more exciting than working towards a great ambition. There is only one way you will discover what kind of work you enjoy and what you would like to get out of your work and that is by taking a first job and learning from that. Once you are engaged in the world of work you will discover what you enjoy doing and build up an idea of what you want to get by doing it.

Do not worry if you have no master plan relating to your career. The workplace offers an incredible number of opportunities and you are in the best position to exploit them. In a diverse workplace there is nothing to stop you from trying out all kinds of different work, workplaces and practices. If you remain open to experience you will learn from everything you do and gradually you will be able to identify a career path.

MAKING CAREER DECISIONS

DREAMS

- what is your lifelong ambition?
- is it attainable?
- what aspects of your dream do you find most attractive?
- what other activities meet these attractions?

WISHES

- where do you see yourself in 5, 10 or 20 years' time?
- will you have a family?
- what lifestyle do you want?
- what area of work will you be in?
- do you need to prioritise these wishes?

DEVELOPING YOUR SKILLS BASE

- what skills do you have that you enjoy using?
- what skills do you have that are in demand?
- what skills would you like to have or to develop?
- what activities will meet these demands?

THE LAST RESORT

- try out any activity and learn as much as you can from the experience

THE BALANCE

- will you work to live or live to work?

HOW TO GET WHAT YOU NEED

Identifying your first move in the world of work and assessing your skills will indicate any additional qualifications or skills you require. You may be able to pick up these skills from the workplace or you may need them prior to employment. There are many ways you can secure new skills and many open and flexible learning courses that you can use in order to find the method of learning that best suits your learning style and lifestyle.

Further academic study can be attractive but make sure of your reasons for continuing in education. It may be necessary to the work you want to do. You may want to teach your subject at a higher level or continue to research an undergraduate interest. Research degrees can take four or five years to complete. Your research may form the start of a career in further education. Study may be full- or part-time, arranged around other pursuits or even around a job. You may be able to get outside commercial interest in your work, guaranteeing financial support for its duration and employment on completion. Further qualifications attract higher starting salaries but only if your specialist knowledge is useful in the job market. The narrower your field of knowledge, the less likely you will be able to apply it to your work.

Some students continue in full-time education because they do not know what to do in the outside world. Postponing your entrance to the job market by taking a qualification you neither want nor need can be more damaging than working in a job you discover is not suitable for you. Your experience of work may indicate a subject which you could research in the future. Work enables you to see how academic theory relates to practice in terms of production techniques and management ideas. Once you have experienced this you may want to go back to the classroom for further study. Staying within an institution with minimum contact with the outside world will not prepare you for the disciplines of a commercial career.

Conversion courses now exist to enable graduates to enter industries alien to their original degree discipline. Arts graduates can take computer training courses preparing them for a career in information technology. Graduates of any discipline can take a conversion course to do law, a path which remains popular in spite of the consequent waiting list to gain qualifying articles. Entering the teaching profession is also open to everyone after a further year of study to gain a Post Graduate Certificate of Education (PGCE).

Vocational qualifications of any description will enhance your chances of getting work. There are courses for almost every job and skill in any industry. There are courses that improve general work skills, which are useful regardless of profession. Being proficient in short-hand or with a certain computer package may give you the edge over other candidates. There are also courses for the self-employed and entrepreneurs establishing new businesses handling areas such as tax, cash flow and accounting.

Courses are available through many establishments, from local colleges, industry representative bodies to private schools. You will find such courses advertised in the local and national press, at the Careers Service and at job centres. Open learning and flexible learning mean you can select the method of study which suits you best. Distance learning, information technology, evening courses and short, intensive courses are available in subjects from accountancy to television presentation. You may be able to access these courses free if you are out of work or financially pressured. The education supplier should be able to point you in the direction of supporting funds. In all cases speak to someone who has recently completed the course and make sure it will give you the skills you need and is worth your effort, time and money.

You may find your employer requires you to study for professional exams. Some companies will pay for the right individual to be trained in the technical side of a job. They employ people on the basis of their aptitude and personality and then help them to acquire the necessary knowledge and skills on the job. Retailers and public relations companies are keen on marketing examinations and there are a whole host of management-related qualifications, from personnel to financial disciplines. Gaining these qualifications can be extremely hard work especially as study is in your own time, usually after a full day's work.

Many employers organise recruiting days or weekends, during which candidates undergo a number of different tests to analyse their mental abilities and working methods and to get an idea of their personality. Psychometric testing includes exercises in textual analysis, mental arithmetic, receptivity to ideas and negotiating skills. There may be group exercises where applicants are given a problem to resolve among themselves, either through discussion or physical activity. They can be unsettling to participate in, as it is difficult to know exactly what the recruiters are looking for. The process is designed to pick out applicants who will best fit into the organisation's working culture, so there is no right or wrong way of completing the tests. You need to relax and show off your talents as well as you can to give a clear idea of who you are. It can be a good idea to rehearse some of these tests before being thrown in at the deep end and the Careers Service run such training days, or will know where such workshops exist.

Experience in the workplace may be more important to your employer than further study. On the job training can take many forms and give you many transferable skills. You may set your sights on an administrative job for a large international company but find they want staff with relevant experience. Gaining a job in administration for a smaller firm in a similar industry or a firm of equal size in a different industry will help you on your way.

Every qualification you gain, no matter how vocational will have transferable elements you can bring to your next working situation. A management theory may provide a theoretical model which you can apply to the organisation of a production process. Typing skills may be extremely useful in a management position. General working skills such as self-discipline, time management and communication are used and developed in every kind of employment. In some cases good time keeping and efficiency are of more value than any number of creative ideas.

Work experience or under-employment can give useful insights into an industry or company and indicate how you can enter the profession at a higher level. Finding a mentor or guru further on in the industry may help you decide the skills and experience you need. You may try to duplicate their working style and career path or you may be able to get personal advice and coaching from that person. At work you may have access to specialist equipment and computer packages. You may not use them as part of your day-to-day work but can still gain valuable experience using the equipment at other times. Arrangements like these show initiative and enthusiasm on your part, which employers will admire and which will open further career opportunities to you.

Lifelong learning is a skill that everyone in the workplace needs if they are to stay employable into the future. Learning is part of being a professional worker. If you believe you know all you will ever need to know for your profession, you will stagnate and become bored. Employers are unlikely to take on a new recruit who tells them at interview where they are going wrong in running the company. Companies and organisations need learners who will get to grips with the business quickly and thoroughly; learners who can comprehend new ideas and techniques, apply them to the workplace and exploit them to the good of the company. This way a company will keep its competitive edge and you will progress through the workplace.

As well as lifelong learning you will need lifelong careers guidance. You will be able to provide some of this for yourself through self-assessment and by periodically re-evaluating your aims. You will need some external help in developing an objective account of your skills and position and to make suggestions on how to approach the future. Only by consciously analysing your position will you be aware of times when your priorities have changed and when you need to change what you are doing in order to address them. You cannot directly compare your activities with those of your contemporaries because your career paths and priorities will be different. You will not gain sufficient objectivity by referring to only one source. It is only by making use of the full range of career resources and maintaining up-to-date knowledge of your workplace that you will appreciate the skills you have and the opportunities available to you.

SUMMARY

WORKING SKILLS CAN BE DEVELOPED THROUGH:

- further academic qualifications
- vocational and skills-led courses and qualifications
- distance and open learning centres
- employer-sponsored courses
- recruitment exercises
- work experience
- lifelong learning
- objective careers planning

CONCLUSION

The shift from long-term job security to short-term contracts is one of which all professionals need to be aware. Indeed, the number of workers currently experiencing this shift either through choice or necessity mean few people do not know someone who is now working in this way. Those who make the transition from traditional employment will have experience of work and know what certain jobs demand. They will be familiar with working practices and know the discipline, energy and commitment required to operate in the workplace. They will be able to key into opportunities because they know what needs doing and, more importantly, who needs it doing. It is this knowledge that will lead to continual work and that graduates must gain as soon as possible.

There is no reason for being despondent about the prospects facing you. Work is still there. There is no lack of economic activity and in some areas you can find long-term employment and employers who will invest in you and develop your skills over a period of time. While fiercely competitive, today's workplace is one of opportunity and freedom rather than one where you must decide what you want to do for the rest of your working life. Decisions that you take now are not the be-all and end-all. Working in one industry for a few years before moving your skills to a completely different area is far more attractive than preparing yourself for forty years of slogging your way up the corporate ladder. Some employers expect graduate recruits to move on within 3–5 years and it is quite legitimate for you to try out an industry or position just to find out what it's like.

The barriers that used to separate what you did for a living from the rest of your life have broken down. Work was traditionally something that occurred away from home, something employees could not wait to get away from on Friday. Working from home means that physical demarcation is disintegrating. Creating your own career allows you to integrate the two areas of life to your own preference rather than trying to fit leisure activities around an employer-set timetable.

What the new structure can lack is a long-term dependable income. This does not prevent you from ever achieving a certain standard of living or material wealth but does affect the way you plan your future. There are no automatic progressions so you must create the opportunities that meet your needs.

Employability is a skill all workers must develop. This means maintaining the right skills and attitudes for the work available. Graduates who have yet to prove themselves in the workplace need to develop their own readiness to enter the world of work. Four factors affect this. They are attainment, self-reliance skills, the ability to learn and mobility.

As a graduate you have already achieved the level of attainment necessary to enter the job market at a professional level. However, you may need further qualifications – academic or vocational training – to enter your profession. Be aware that attainment can exclude you from the workplace.

Self-reliance skills have already helped you to complete a college course and take part in many other activities at the same time. The organisational skills that enabled you to organise your college life must now be taken one stage further to run your employed life. An employer used to provide training and development support, remuneration, recreation and social activities. You will need to create these structures for yourself, especially if you are in a small company or are self-employed. The ability to assess your direction and how your working life fits into this will shape a successful career.

Self-reliance skills include a flexible approach to work and a breadth of knowledge that can be applied in a variety of situations. Specialist knowledge can be the key to a lucrative career but finding the right employment situation in which to use it can be difficult. A flexible approach means you can create your career to meet lifestyle or skill-based ambitions. This is a far more realistic way to arrange a career than to single out a specific job.

Careers are unique to individuals. This has always been the case but today there may not be anyone who works in the same way as you. You could feel a lack of support or identity from contemporaries and other workers. The camaraderie and sense of belonging that came with the traditional job is difficult to generate among the short-term employed and in order to compensate, professionals need a high level of self-confidence. Help and support can be gained from individuals in similar circumstances but contentment lies in the satisfaction of your own desires and needs.

Everyone in employment needs the ability to learn. The speed of change in all areas of life is phenomenal and the worker who refuses to change in order to accommodate this is the one who will be out of work. Lifelong learning recognises that everyone must continue to develop their skills no matter who they are or what they do. Even top level management and chief executives cannot afford to think their position makes them inviolable. They need continuous development as much as anybody else. If mistakes are made at this level the repercussions affect the entire company.

Lifelong learning also recognises that gaining knowledge and developing a career is a lifelong activity. You cannot walk out of college and become chief executive of a multinational company. You need substantial experience to gain the necessary skills. If you are creating a career that will achieve a certain position you will know the time it will take for you to learn how to do that job. Further and higher education are not passports to lucrative employment, but simply stepping stones along your career path; experiences from which you have gained more than an academic qualification.

Mobility is psychological as well as geographical. You need to accept movement between industries, positions of responsibility, hierarchies and even between your own priorities. Geographical mobility decreases with time as families are established and children go to school. Relocation can also be difficult for households where both partners are working when one has to sacrifice their work for the sake of the other's career.

Three principal factors lead to failure to get employment or the loss of employment. Firstly, you will fail if you are not clear about what your aims are. If you don't know what you want to do or why you need to do something you cannot make any decisions regarding employment. Taking employment must satisfy either short- or long-term goals. It could support activities outside work or move you towards a specific job or lifestyle in the future. It could satisfy a dream or give you a new skill. On leaving college your only reason for taking employment may be to pay off your overdraft. This is a valid short-term reason and once engaged in an activity you may discover a longer-term or more personal reason to take you on to the next point in your career.

The second reason for failure is that you do not want to do the job strongly enough. You will lose employment either because you are bored with what you are doing and so leave of your own accord, or because your employer detects you are not committed and replaces you. You must convince yourself, and your employer, that you are the right person for the job and this conviction is based on the reason for doing the job in the first place. If you are a reluctant worker consider what aspect of the work deters you. This can be used in a positive way to arrive at more suitable work. You may dislike shop work because you do not like dealing with the public, in which case your next step could be to find an office based job.

The final reason for failure is that you do not know what you need to know. You may be enthusiastic about becoming an air-traffic controller but you don't know how to get into the profession. You may want to work in advertising but you don't know what the culture is like so cannot make an effective application. To work in any area you must carry out some research. You need to build up some idea of what working in that industry is like and recruiters will look for evidence of interest in the industry in your application and interview.

You cannot expect everything to fall into place the moment you walk out of college. A common experience is to be unemployed immediately but to find employment within a year. Even if you have a firm idea of where you are going and the work you are taking there are many unexpected influences that will affect you over the first few months outside college. Being a student can be a fairly relaxed and certainly a social activity: being employed can be extremely tiring, reduce your recreation time and put you under a great deal of pressure. Until you engage with the job market you will not know what is on offer or how you will fit into working life. If you really have no idea where you want to work then think how much more you will know after one week in any job. Taking a temporary retail sales job will immediately tell you whether you like working with people, handling money, managing stock, your fellow workers or working with the product you are selling.

As your experience grows your work-related ambitions will alter, and as you get older your life-style needs and expectations will be revised. You must not be afraid of changing your priorities or lifestyle to meet these. The competitive nature of the job market means many people are scared of losing their work and finding something new. If you remain flexible and self-reliant in your working arrangements you will always find suitable new opportunities. In traditional working structures, all employees can expect is an annual increase in remuneration and promotion when the company can afford it or when their immediate superior decides to move on. If you create your own career you can decide when to change your employment and that change can bring a completely different working environment and set of challenges.

A career really only exists in the past tense. It is a record of what you have done and achieved. If you consider what has already happened to you, you will find the most interesting and significant events occurred not when your expectations were met but when the unexpected happened. Careers frequently take surprising twists as pre-planned events fail to materialise and new opportunities suddenly appear. Your best career move may not be promotion from supervisor to line manager but when a friend tells you what his friend does for a living and you realise he's describing the job you want. There may be times when it feels as if nothing is happening; when you are under-employed with a Christmas job and have no prospects for the future. The experience is so awful it spurs you into deciding precisely what you want to do for a living. As a result, you walk out of work one day and apply for a vocational course, which leads you into truly satisfying full-time employment.

This is not arguing against making any plans at all, but highlighting the need to be constantly aware of the possibilities open to you. Creating your career is about creating the opportunities that will lead you in the direction in which you want to go. You can create those opportunities at any time regardless of your current employment situation. You do not need to rigorously map out your progression, but if you have an idea of where you're going you will find it easy to make decisions relating to where and how you work. Well defined aims and strong motivation make everything you do contribute towards that goal. You will pick up relevant skills automatically from every working experience and find job satisfaction in whatever you do. Pursuing or executing work half-heartedly or worrying you're doing the wrong thing not only jeopardises your employment but prevents you learning from the current experience and exploring and exploiting the opportunities it offers.

No book can prescribe a career path for an individual. The impetus for taking employment can only come from you. There are no rules governing which activity is best for you and nothing to limit what you can do. It may be years before you find the activity you regard as your true vocation but that does not stop you from engaging in work now and enjoying employment and the benefits it brings.

No job is forever. Your first position may simply provide work experience with which to decide your next move. Alternatively, it may be the first rung on that organisation's corporate ladder. Approach the job market positively and inquisitively. Never presume you know what an industry or job is like or that you know what opportunities are available in one particular area. Do not allow yourself to be side-tracked into an activity you do not feel committed to. Above all enjoy what you do. If you establish good reasons for your working activities and create a career that addresses these, you will find you naturally acquire the necessary working skills and will always be able to access satisfying employment opportunities.

ARE YOU READY FOR WORK?

- **Attainment**
  do you have the necessary education and training for work?
- **Self-reliance skills**
  are you flexible enough to use your skills in a variety of situations?
- **Ability to learn**
  will you take on new ideas in the workplace and are you committed to lifelong learning?
- **Mobility**
  are you willing to travel to take work and willing to change your preconceptions of the workplace?

THE KEY TO WORK

- **Know your aims**
  What are you working towards? What will you achieve in the short term? What will you achieve in the long term?
- **Make sure you want the work and that other people know you want the work**
  How does this work reflect your aims and contribute to achieving them?
- **Know what you need to know**
  Research your area of work. Make sure it is the right work for you and that you stand a realistic chance of working there.

REMEMBER!

Remain sensitive to the changes around you; changes in the workplace and changes to your own demands out of life.
Remain open to chance but dedicated to your direction.

INDEX

Also available from Kogan Page

Kogan Page 'Careers in' Series

'Essential information at affordable prices'
   Times Educational Supplement

These practical and inexpensive books are packed with useful information and sound advice on a wide variety of professions and careers, from accountancy to working with young people. They discuss types of jobs available within a particular field as well as training and qualifications needed. Written by experts, these handy paperbacks are essential reading for all careers advisers, school and college leavers, graduates or anyone considering a career change. Please phone 0171 278 0433 if you would like more information on *Careers in*...

Accountancy, 5th edn
Architecture, 4th edn
Banking and Finance, 4th edn
Catering and Hotel Management,
   4th edn
Environmental Conservation, 6th edn
Fashion, 3rd edn
Film and Video, 4th edn
Hairdressing and Beauty Therapy, 7th edn
Journalism, 7th edn
The Law, 7th edn
*Marketing, Advertising and Public
   Relations,* 5th edn
Medicine, Dentistry and Mental Health,
   7th edn

Nursing and Related Professions,
   6th edn
Police Force, 4th edn
Published and Bookselling, 2nd edn
Retailing, 5th edn
Secretarial and Office Work, 7th edn
Social Work, 5th edn
Television and Radio, 6th edn
The Theatre, 5th edn
Travel Industry, 5th edn
Using Languages, 7th edn
Working Outdoors, 6th edn
Working with Animals, 7th edn
*Working with Children and Young
   People,* 6th edn